Prairie
Rock
Garden

Donna Balzer

Red Deer Press

The Publishers
Red Deer Press
Room 813, MacKimmie Library Tower
2500 University Drive NW
Calgary Alberta Canada T2N 1N4

Credits
Cover design by Boldface Technologies
Text design by Dennis Johnson
Typesetting by Amy Becker
Printed and bound in Canada by Friesens for Red Deer Press

Acknowledgments
Financial support provided by the Department of Canadian Heritage and by the Alberta Foundation for the Arts, a beneficiary of the Lottery Fund of the Government of Alberta.

COMMITTED TO THE DEVELOPMENT OF CULTURE AND THE ARTS

Canadian Cataloguing in Publication Data
Balzer, Donna, 1956–
The prairie rock garden
(Prairie garden books)
ISBN 0-88995-195-0
1. Rock gardens—Prairie Provinces. I. Title. II. Series.
SB459.B34 1999   635.9'672'09712   C99-910095-5

5 4 3 2 1

For my parents,
Della and Harvey Balzer

Author Acknowledgments

Writing a book is essentially a process of elimination. It is possible to find great ideas everywhere you look, but deciding which ideas will get the beginner from paper to practice is difficult. I thank the many members of CRAGS (Calgary Rock and Alpine Garden Society) for their combined ideas and wisdom, which provided guidance for this book. First President of CRAGS, Sheila Paulson, contributed much to this book, especially to the extensive plant list. Susanna Barlem, ornamentals gardener at the Calgary Zoo Botanical Garden, was also invaluable for feedback.

In horticulture it didn't take me long to realize that it was one thing to know a fact and quite another to *show* it to others. A great photo can often better convince a new gardener to try a plant or plant combination than any number of words. In this regard I thank professional photographer George Webber, who guided me gently past beginner status in photography. George made sure I was *seeing* the good and leaving out the bad.

Although I never intended to write in any detail about geology, the very nature of rock gardening meant I needed to be briefed on the scientific side of rocks. Rocks aren't just a pretty backdrop in the garden. They contribute their color, texture and even chemical properties to the landscape, and without the guidance of retired geologist and geophysicist Desmond Allen I wouldn't have been able to fully understand and convey the prairie rock information included here.

Many people opened their gardens and allowed me to take photos or offered their own photos for use in this book. Thanks go to Zoltan Gulyas, Rodney Shaver, Cliff and Sheila Paulson, Joey Stewart, Llyn Strelau, Peter Braun, Ken Girard, Shirley Scott, Margaret Brown, Pat and Neil Boyle, the Metzlaff gardens (in Calgary and Invermere), Tom and Diane McCabe, Ed Garvin and Wilhelm Roth. Bill Quayle is not a gardener, but he willingly supplied photos of natural areas and plants.

Finally I need to thank the person who made math in the garden easy for me. Peter Schill, Math Department Head at George McDougall High School in Airdrie, helped me sort out the practical math questions gardeners face every time they order soil or mulch for their gardens. He worked with me to develop the chart included on page 148.

Thanks to all of these generous contributors I have completed this second book—a prairie rock garden primer—and am thrilled to share the results with fellow gardeners.

Contents

The Joy of Rock Gardens

MY FATHER WAS SO HORRIFIED when he saw rocks in my first garden that I could hardly admit I had paid for them. After his many years of farming, which involved plenty of rock picking, he could not imagine why anyone would use rocks on purpose anywhere—let alone buy them. But for gardeners rocks can be a thing of beauty, and all prairie gardens, sloped or flat, are ideal candidates for rock gardens. Flowers alone, whether perennials or annuals, leave a garden looking dead all winter. Trees and shrubs alone don't have the same dynamic impact as a garden with flowers. Rocks by themselves are just inert hard skeletons in the landscape, but combining all three elements—flowers, woody plants and rocks—provides broad four-season interest in the prairie garden.

Rock gardens combine hardy perennials and rock to create beautiful natural-looking scenes.
(GARDEN BY KEN GIRARD)

7

TOP: *Combine geology and botany in new ways to draw the eye through small spaces.*
BOTTOM: *A trough made of porous cement and filled with alpine plants allows rock gardening in even the smallest of spaces.*
(ILLUSTRATION BY KATHERINE VINISH)

Exactly what is a rock garden? Is it designed of rocks with plants in mind, or is it designed of plants with rocks in mind? You decide. Geologists who garden may choose their rock first—for color, form or sentimental value. Plant people may choose their rock last to complement the plants they have selected. Rock gardens mean different things to different people, and most rock gardeners will use a variety of methods to choose the best combination of plants and rocks for their gardens. It doesn't have to be a scientific process.

The only thing rock gardens ever seem to have in common is the combination of geology and botany in a single space. However many and varied the interpretations of rock gardens may be, most gardeners agree that rock gardens most often make use of compact and slow-growing species found at alpine elevations or arctic latitudes. From that point, new gardeners will bring their personal interpretation of the term *rock garden* to the discussion, and from there the results will be anything but predictable.

For me, a rock garden is a place to celebrate the beauty of the mountain and prairie landscape. All too often, behind perfectly manicured lawns and hedges, our urban landscapes shut us off from the beauty of this natural scene. I've used my rock garden to bring a bit of the wild inside my garden.

Rock gardens are as variable as gardeners, whose imaginations result in everything from tiny single-rock trough or container gardens on city balconies ·to massive 50-tonne rubble piles on country acreages. Taste and style run from formal plantings along stone walls to informal creations taking inspiration from the many naturally occurring rock outcrops within the prairie landscape and the Rocky Mountains.

The variability of rock garden interpretations leads to a question that is controversial to some:

Whatever the motive that brings gardeners to rock gardening, they quickly discover the practical and aesthetic advantages of rock gardens on the prairies. One of the key practical advantages is their suitability to the prairie environment. Rock garden plants are naturally adapted to thrive in the extremes of the prairie climate, which can include pounding hail, few frost-free days and low precipitation. Among the hardy rock garden plants, none is as adaptable to changes in temperature and climate as compact mountain species. When hailstorms, for instance, leave the broad-leaved and statuesque perennial border delphiniums *(Delphinium* x *belladonna* cvs.) shredded and bedraggled, the smaller rockery Chinese delphiniums *(Delphinium grandiflorum* cvs.) can emerge relatively unscathed because their leaves are already finely cut and the plant is lower and rounder in form than the taller, more vulnerable garden hybrids. Similarly, while a tomato may need 120 frost-free days to set and ripen fruit, small mountain plants such as moss campion *(Silene acaulis)*, Douglasia *(Douglasia montana)* and draba *(Draba* spp.) need as few as 10 to 20 frost-free days to bloom gloriously.

Many rock garden plants have evolved in drought-prone climates, so they are ideal for our low-humidity, low-rainfall prairie conditions. Unlike plants with origins in wetter

climates, species growing naturally on a steep mountainside, such as dwarf species tulips *(Tulipa tarda)*, benefit from spring runoff and spring rains but go dormant later in the dry heat. Other plants such as the many drought-tolerant cultivars of sedums *(Sedum* cvs.) or hens and chicks *(Sempervivum* cvs.) have succulent leaves that hold water to protect them through dry spells.

Rock in the garden serves practical purposes as well. Sloped sites especially need the physical presence of rock to break the fall of rain and prevent soil erosion. These natural stabilizers anchor the earth and plants on the slope and allow the water to settle long enough to permit plant rooting.

One of the funniest gardens I have ever viewed broke many rock garden rules to repeat a single rock form —painstakingly collected heart-shaped rocks. Low ground covers were chosen so that plants would not hide the shape of the feature rocks.

Draba (Draba spp.) are native to the Rocky Mountains and are ideally suited to cool climate gardens. They need as few as 10–20 frost free days to bloom.

Douglasia (Douglasia montana), an alpine plant from Montana and Wyoming, pops into bloom after just a few warm days in spring.

and go as quickly as the next unexpected blizzard or Chinook, rock in itself adds aesthetic value to the garden. Snow piled on rock creates beautiful forms and elevations in the winter landscape. Snow receding from a lichen-covered boulder in early spring reveals brilliant orange colonizing patches of life even before small plants are revealed and revived.

Flat landscapes especially benefit from the natural jagged and unifying beauty of rock. If the view across a flat garden is toward another flat surface such as a bowling-green–style lawn, the addition of rock to the planting beds will boost the visual impact and create a more permanent look.

Rock gardeners need not despair that their gardens will lack color. Both rocks and plantings provide a wide range to choose from. Rock colors range from pale grey and black to pink and green. Depending on their location they may additionally develop beautiful colonies of lichens or moss. Foliage colors run from blue and green to dark bur-

Yet another key practical advantage of rock gardens is that they are relatively maintenance free once established. Gardeners with busy lifestyles will especially appreciate that, beyond occasionally topping up the garden with mulch or adding newly discovered plants, little ongoing labor is required.

In addition to practical benefits, rock gardening has many aesthetic advantages. On the prairies, where our spring can last a day or a month, and where winter can come

The common name hens and chicks is applied to two genera: Sempervivum and Jovibarba. Both are heat and drought tolerant. Their beautiful texture and color come from compact rosettes of fleshy leaves.

gundy and gold, and woody deciduous shrubs also add brilliant autumn leaf color. Bloom colors range from white and yellow to rich pink and vibrant blue. In fact, some of the most brilliant colors available in the plant world are features of rock garden plants.

Throughout this book on prairie rock gardening, I'll share step-by-step design, construction and maintenance ideas for rock gardens sure to please any taste. Photographs supply additional guidance and inspiration. Chapter 1, "Designing Rock Gardens," helps you understand the rock garden as a separate entity, or as part of a bigger overall space, by reviewing the basic design elements contributing to garden

Species tulips such as Tulipa tarda go dormant in the heat of the summer in order to survive.

success. Chapter 2, "Selecting Plants for the Rock Garden," guides you through the process that will bring your design to life. Chapter 3, "Selecting Rock for the Rock Garden," helps you choose the type of rock to complement your design and plant selections. Chapter 4, "Constructing the Rock Garden," takes you step-by-step through the construction process. Chapter 5, "Planting the Rock Garden," provides planting guidance, and Chapter 6, "Seasonal Care of Rock Gardens," guides you through the maintenance process season by season.

If there is a single simple thing prairie gardeners can do to pick up and explode the interest in their

Lichen-covered boulders provide year-round seasonal interest in the rock garden.

landscapes it is to incorporate rock. If you have already made room for a rose garden and a water garden (the two books written previously in this Prairie Garden Books series), it might be time to haul out the gear again and begin building your prairie rock garden.

CHAPTER 1

Designing Rock Gardens

ROCK IS THE GREAT EQUALIZER. A garden designed of flowers only will be dull in the winter. A garden of pure evergreens will have winter color but will have a static look all summer when other gardens glow. A garden combining annuals, perennials and woody plants, however, will provide interest throughout the seasons. If there is an addition that can make this ideal four-season plant collection even better, it is to incorporate rock into the garden plan. Rock is zero maintenance and adds interesting contour changes, continuous textural interest and color not just from the rocks themselves but from the lichens and mosses that frequently grow on them. The use of rock throughout the landscape brings elements of harmony and permanence to the garden that are visible year-round.

A well-designed rock garden provides year-round interest as color, form and texture change throughout the seasons.

15

Several acres of landscaping— including this alpine garden— are contained within the University of Alberta's Devonian Botanic gardens in Edmonton. Large sweeping beds are mulched with gravel and planted with hardy evergreens and rock garden perennials.

Determining a Style

Rock gardening is practiced on all continents, but at its best it is interpreted differently depending on naturally available rocks and plants. Some of the most widely known and easily recognized rock interpretations have been made in Japanese, British and American gardens. A Japanese rock garden, although inspired by nature, is a minimalist space dedicated to tightly controlled plants and rock patterns. It rarely includes distracting items such as lush floral displays or loosely arranged plant groupings. Even the rock is raked and measured. In contrast, British-style gardens take advantage of organic soils, emergent rock and high humidity to feature lush foliage with overlapping textures, layers and flowering seasons. The British rock garden is a complicated and delicate artform requiring high maintenance for success in our harsh, dry, prairie climate. The American-style rock garden borrows design elements freely from around the world. It will often, for example, use a Japanese-style arrangement of rock in a lush, British-style flower setting that includes hardy plants of Himalayan origin. Each style makes effective use of plant and rock combinations that are inspired by the local environment.

If you are tempted to re-create in your prairie landscape a garden style inspired by another country, you should consider if the style suits your site, if it meets your maintenance expectations and, most importantly, if it makes geological common sense. If there is no chance you'll see a particular rock combination or plant pattern in your local landscape, you should think twice before combining it in your rock garden. For example, fol-

lowing the Japanese tradition of incorporating single vertical rocks standing alone or as part of a planting bed will look odd in your prairie garden for good reason: there is no context for it in the prairie environment except for glacial erratics, and these look out of place even though produced by ancient glacial action. Originally, there was an inspiring natural Japanese rock outcrop that triggered this unusual use of rock and raked gravel in the Oriental garden. But North American copies of this garden style are so far from their original natural inspiration that they seem unnatural. If there is no precedent in the local landscape, the garden picture you create will not seem appropriate.

Yet another style of rock gardening is found in the formal garden with its highly structured, geometrically balanced plantings of beds, terraces and walls. If this style suits

TOP: Take your camera or sketch pad along to record scenes in nature such as this natural rock garden in Colorado.

BOTTOM: Or capture scenes like this natural rock garden in the mountains of Alberta.

your site, maintenance expectations and desires, then go ahead. But if you want to re-create a slice of nature by designing a rock garden

Wilhelm Roth has created an entire alpine rock garden within a portable trough. He chose featherstone, a type of volcanic rock, because its light weight will allow the trough to be moved from time to time.

suited to our prairie and mountain landforms and naturally occurring rock, visit nature first. Your investigation might take you sightseeing along the rocky banks of a river valley, the outcroppings of a coulee, the sweeping view of the foothills or mountains, the hoodoos of the badlands or even the deep shade within woodland areas. Any of these may be a source of inspiration for a rock garden that makes sense in your environment and is specifically suited to the prairie climate. If you want to construct a small trough garden on an apartment balcony, you might look for examples of compact species on an alpine slope or succulents within a sunlit coulee. If you're planning a rock garden on a sweep-

ing farm or acreage property, you might take inspiration from a rock slide that may take many tons of Rundle rock to complete. Between the two extremes are as many variations as there are gardeners. Take your camera or sketch pad on hikes and look for scenes that will give you a natural reference point when you start constructing. Take note as well of the soil conditions supporting the plants you desire.

Themes from Nature

It is best to design a rock garden by imitating a scene from nature rather than imitating another gardener's idea of nature. Just like photocopies get worse with every copy of the last copy, a great garden can

hardly ever be created by imitating a vision of nature interpreted by another gardener. The following themes represent some of the more common scenes from the natural environment that may inspire and guide your prairie rock garden design. They are not meant to represent strict rules. Rather they are suggestions to trigger inspiration.

The River Cutaway

In a cutbank along a river, the rocks are sharp and protrude erratically out of the exposed soil while the plants trail over and between them. Erosion has cut away the soil between rocks, and the effect is dramatic. Home garden sites suited to this naturally occurring style will be sloping and will feature a constructed stream. The rocks are then placed at every twist and turn as though the stream were following a natural path.

The Prairie Coulee

This little slice of prairie is much like a river cutaway except running water is absent. Distinct layers of rock, usually sandstone, run horizontally across the coulee, starting on one slope and extending across to the other. To re-create this effect on a sloping garden site, the rocks are sloped in horizontal planes. The coulee-style garden is a great place to use drought-tolerant plants such as our prairie native yucca *(Yucca filamentosa)* and cactus *(Opuntia fragilis)*.

Coulees and prairie grasslands are home to prickly pear cactus. These natural scenes may provide the needed inspiration for a prairie coulee rock garden. (PHOTO BY BILL QUAYLE)

LEFT: A true prairie native is the prickly pear cactus (Opuntia polyacantha), which is found growing wild across the prairies. (PHOTO BY BILL QUAYLE)

RIGHT: A natural prairie coulee may inspire a unique prairie rock garden with local plants for your own backyard.

BOTTOM: A small garden stream uses both river rock and slab rock (sandstone) to create a natural-looking stream in Joey Stewart's tiny backyard rock garden.

The Fell Field

At the foot of an avalanche chute in the mountains, boulders may be piled irregularly as if tipped out of a dump truck. The rocks will be blocky and sharp-angled because they have slipped off the side of the mountain and come crashing down the slope. The plants will spring in enterprising fashion from tiny cracks between the rocks. This style is best suited to the base of a hill in a yard with a steep pitch or dramatic change of grade. Small pruned evergreen shrubs such as Ohlendorffii spruce *(Picea abies* 'Ohlendorffii') can be incorporated above the garden to complete this scene inspired by nature.

Slabs and Faces

Often in the mountains, tiny alpines, spilling rock willow and tight mounds of plants are found clinging to cracks in small crevices on shear or steeply sloping cliff faces. To re-create this effect in a steeply raised bed, flat rocks may be tipped on their sides with just the smallest planting pockets left between them. Compact plants such as fleabane *(Erigeron compositus),* penstemon *(Penstemon albertinus* or *Penstemon hirsutus* "Pygmaeus"), douglasia *(Douglasia montana),* mountain avens *(Dryas octopetala),* spring gentian *(Gentiana verna),* or blue fescue *(Festuca glauca)* may be used among the cracks created between rock slabs.

Rock Cracks and Crevices

Within a larger mountain scene are many closeup views of rock lifted in slivered layers and fissures often created when frost cracks the rock. The gravel that gradually fills the upward-tilting shelves is later colonized by the tiniest alpines, ground covers and mounded plants. Gardens modeled after cracks and crevices are narrow in profile and composed of flat sharp-edged rocks. To create a crevice garden, relatively flat rocks are tilted into the slope of a raised bed or natural slope, and the space between is filled with specially prepared soil. The plants are then set between the tilted rocks and mulched with fine gravel to imitate scree, which is the loose gravel

Prairie plants such as yucca (Yucca filamentosa) and native prickly pear cactus (Opuntia spp.) are combined in Sheila Paulson's varied prairie rock garden.

The beginnings of a fell field–style rock garden, where a large garden space and changing elevation make the scene ring true to nature. (DESIGN BY ED GARVIN)

A natural rock crevice on a grand scale can be seen from the water within Montana's Glacier National Park.

and small rock found at the base of a rock wall in a mountain or at the edge of a glacier. Expect to find moss campion *(Silene acaulis)*, phlox *(Phlox hoodii* and *Phlox subulata)*, primula (such as *Primula marginata* or *Primula hirsuta)*, saxifrage (such as *Saxifraga bronchialis* or *Saxifraga oppositifolia)* in the spaces created.

Exposed Surface Rock

A steeply sloping hill may be littered with rock that has gradually become visible after years of erosion. These views are composed of fairly modest-sized lichen-covered rocks emerging from the soil and surrounded by various hardy dwarf shrubs and flowers. The overall effect of an exposed-rock style in

A crevice garden provides numerous planting opportunities and an ideal alpine garden habitat.

the prairie garden is an open space dotted with color and plants of compact form. Full-sized shrubs are avoided because these would dwarf the small rocks and minimize their overall impact.

Rocky Mountain or Fieldstone Berms

Natural berms occur when large numbers of field stones are dropped by receding glaciers. The spaces between the stones are colonized by plants at lower elevations. Re-creating a mountain berm scene occasionally might mean hauling in rocks of mammoth proportion, but successful interpretations may be developed with little more than blocky square-edged limestone or granite forming a small rise in the landscape. Larger slab-rock gardens also can be created from long thin blocks, and fieldstone can be stacked into piles. Fieldstones will

Manmade or natural? This crevice garden is exacting in its detail and design.

have soft rounded edges, but after years of exposure they will have the added character of colorful lichens.

Rock Features, Walls and Troughs

Cracks in large rocks in the alpine scene often become occupied by compact hardy alpines, an effect that can be re-created in large rock

In nature, a cliff face is sharply sheared—plants hang precariously from the cracks created.

Cliff faces may be recreated in city gardens to duplicate nature's best efforts. Here, horticultural species such as blue chip juniper (Juniperus horizontalis 'Blue Chip') fill in for the native horizontal junipers seen wild in the mountains and prairie coulees.

features in the garden and in small trough planters on the patio. In a large rock feature it is possible to chip out a space in which a small plant will look at home. The crack is filled with rock garden soil, leaf mold or composted peat, and a few seeds are sprinkled in. If the chosen plant is succulent or a quick-rooting type such as an auricula primula *(Primula auricula)* or hens and chicks *(Sempervivum* cvs.), a small cutting may be wedged in the crack. The result will be a rock planter with what appears to be natural growth. If the rock is set into soil and especially if it is porous (such as tufa), it will stay moist and support many plants at once.

If the rocks in the garden are too

Lichen-covered rocks and tough drought-tolerant rockery plants combine to create a jewel-box moment in an exposed rock garden.

A natural rocky mountain berm includes rock emerging from the soil. Within this natural scene, plants grow between cracks and between larger open ground spaces—two distinctly different growing zones.

small to support plants by themselves, consider constructing a dry rock wall and setting individual plants between the rock layers. These living walls work best if small plants are laid between rock cracks, preferably at the joints where the rocks butt together. Greater overall success will be achieved if the wall is not very wide so the plant roots initially don't have to grow beyond 10" (25 cm) to reach soil. Eventually even the smallest plant will develop a long root system. If plants are added after the wall is built a crowbar may be used to create a space between layers of rock. A slim-rooted plant is then tucked in place and a small sliver of rock or a wooden stake is used to hold the space until

RIGHT: Planting areas created in cracks in fieldstone or berm gardens are similar in appearance to the crevice garden.

TOP LEFT: Native prairie fleabane (Erigeron compositus) planted in a large rock with a crack looks very natural.

BOTTOM LEFT: Rosenzwerg (also known as Rosyveil saxifrage (Saxifraga x arendsii 'Rozenzwerg') is a low-growing alpine perfect for filling small cracks. It may need replacing every three to five years.

the root fills the area. If the rock wall is part of a rock garden it will look more natural if the rock is not only tilting back into the soil but if the whole rock group tilts away from the horizon.

Plants such as Lewisia *(Lewisia cotyledon* or *Lewisia rediviva)*, pussy-toes *(Antennaria rosea)*, rock jasmine *(Androsace primuloides)*, basket of gold alyssum *(Aurinia saxatalis)* work well spilling over tops of walls or creeping out of cracks between them.

Miniature rock wall features are at risk of drying out in extreme drought (both during winters with little snow and summers with little rain), but the one thing that will never happen in a rock wall is crown rot because drainage is guaranteed. Orienting the garden north or northeast helps to keep the rock face cool and plant dessication is kept to a minimum. Using plants with succulent roots or stems such as bitteroot *(Lewisia* spp.), sedums *(Sedum* spp.) or hens and chicks *(Sempervivum* spp.) will help the rock wall become established and successful.

Rock wall features should not extend to stand-alone rock walls, which are not usually successful on the prairies. Without a soil bank behind the wall to retain moisture, plant crowns gradually dry out completely.

LEFT: Plants fill the cracks and crannies provided in the Strelau–Shaver rock garden.

RIGHT: One of the great trailing plants from Kashmir— Androsace sempervivoides *—literally hangs by its fine stringlike stolons from cracks and crevices in rock walls. Its bright pink flowers are a bonus in early summer.*

BOTTOM: Here plants are added to a rock wall that slopes slightly back into the soil instead of standing free and exposed to air on both sides.

Woodland or Understory Gardens

The woodland or understory rock garden may be a variation of any of the many rock garden types described here with only one difference—shade. The shade in these gardens come from overhead trees or from a north-facing aspect. Simply substitute shade-loving rockery plants as appropriate. Instead of corydalis *(Corydalis* spp.) try sedum *(Hylotelephium* spp.). For dianthus *(Dianthus* spp.) try fern leaf bleeding heart *(Dicentra eximia).* If the garden is very shady, ferns such as fragile fern *(Cystopteris fragilis)* will be the logical substitution for a native cactus such as the prickly pear *(Opuntia* spp.), which would be found growing in a similar but sunnier site.

TOP: A free-standing rock wall is a work of art but will not support plant life in the dry prairie climate.

BOTTOM LEFT: Ramonda (Ramonda myconii) is an unusual member of the African violet family, which—because of its moisture-sensitive hairy leaves—must be grown almost on its side, making it ideally suited to life in a small backfilled rock wall.

BOTTOM RIGHT: The woodland look is reserved for the shady corner of the garden regardless of overall rock garden concept or style. In any area with heavier shade the hardy native fragile fern (Cystopteris fragilis) is at home.

Formal versus Informal Style

A garden designed to maintain the order established by a centrally placed front door is destined to be formal. In a formal garden, the rock type and quantity match almost exactly—not an easy task when using natural materials. The plants also are often aligned along a central axis for symmetrical balance and are trimmed to grow in unison with little side shoots removed as they appear. This ensures that the two sides of the garden match like lions at an entry gate.

Formal rock gardens, like formal gardens of any kind, require more attention to detail in planning and more frequent maintenance over the long term. To keep things as simple as possible in a formal garden, you should choose plants that have relatively even growth habits. There will be no room in the formal garden, for example, for a Koster spruce *(Picea pungens* 'Koster'*)* with its wild and lunging growth habit or

for an independent-looking bristlecone pine *(Pinus aristata)* that can never be enticed to grow in an upright symmetrical form. The formal garden calls for plants such as the very tidy *Dianthus microlepsis* or dwarf grafted sea urchin white pine *(Pinus strobus* 'Sea Urchin'). The reliable uniform shape of the various coral bells *(Heuchera* spp. and cvs.) is also more suited to formal rock gardens than the irregular and random ground covers such as Aubrieta *(Aubrieta* x *cultorum)* or dead nettle *(Lamium maculatum* cvs.). Upright trees like the columnar blue spruce *(Picea pungens* 'Iseli Fastigiate') can be easily maintained in their columnar form, while most free-spreading junipers

Juniperus spp. and cvs.) will need ongoing and determined maintenance to retain a formal shape. One exception is the tightly compact blue star juniper *(Juniperus squatama* 'Blue Star'), which stays in a tight mound.

An informal garden is not to be interpreted as a garden without style. It still makes use of the tried and true elements of good garden design, but it is generally easier to maintain because the plants are not kept clipped or as carefully controlled. The balance is also a little more causal, so the natural variation in plant growth among the same species is not important. While a formal garden may be aligned along the straight

LEFT: A shade tolerant plant in the primula family with delicate nodding flowers in early summer is cortusa (Cortusa mathiola).

RIGHT: An informal trough garden is created within a pre-cast cement planter. This mini-garden in Sheila Paulson's yard illustrates how an entire crevice garden can be built in a space less than 1 yd (1 m) across.

LEFT: An independent-looking bristle-cone pine (Pinus aristata)— especially this dead one seen at a high elevation in Colorado— would not suit a formal garden setting.

RIGHT: This predictable narrow, columnar form of blue spruce (Picea pungens 'Iseli Fastigiate') is very formal in appearance although it could also be used as a point of emphasis in an informal garden.

lines created by a grand entry walk, the informal garden may curve around a fish pool, emerge from behind a grove of evergreens or simply wrap irregularly around the long and straight entry to the home.

The typically straight lines of most urban lots and structures need not dictate a formal garden design. With a little careful planning, there can be a lot of interpretation within the strict boundaries set by pre-existing walkways or structures. For example, the plantings for an informal garden can be contained within straight lines of paving or rock walls.

Selecting the Site

The ideal rock garden site will have good drainage and receive some sun and shade throughout the day. Neither condition may be completely available in the location you

desire, but don't despair. Drainage, especially important in rock gardens, can almost always be improved by creating elevation, and light conditions can often be improved by adding or taking away shade.

If your ideal site is located on a slope, you may need to layer the rocks to reduce the rush of water and resulting soil erosion. If no slope is available, you'll need to plan for some elevation by creating small berms of back-sloping rock, which offer aesthetic and practical benefits. Berms will improve drainage, and because knolls or small swales in the prairie occur naturally, small berms look authentic.

If the garden receives full sun all day, trees or shrubs can be planted near but unrelated to the garden itself. Another option to consider is planting trees or shrubs commonly

found in the natural scene you are using as your model. These woody plants become an extension of the rock garden while adding needed shade. Alternately, the garden can be designed with some change in elevation to create pockets of full or partial shade. The same can be accomplished by orienting the garden so that at least part of the day it shades itself. An east exposure is ideal on the prairies.

If the best location for your rock garden is presently in full shade, you can explore the possibility of removing or pruning trees or shrubs to encourage dappled but not heavy shade. Another option is to enlarge or orient the garden differently so that for part of the day it is in open light. A final option is to select shade-tolerant plants and design a north-face mountain or woodland understory garden. A shade rock garden may include more lichens

and moss and possibly a small stream for interest instead of the full range of rock plants found in brighter alpine environments. Plants suitble to this habitat will thrive in low light and may be grown for their foliage rather than flowers.

More often than not prairie gardeners have to contend with too much light rather than too little when choosing a rock garden location, a problem not typically addressed by gardening book authors from climates with heavy rain and limited sunlight. "An ideal site for a rock garden would be on a gentle slope facing southwest, fully in the open and not overhung by trees," suggests Will Ingwersen in his British book *Alpine and Rock Plants.* This type of orientation allows gardeners in coastal or cloudy climates to approximate an alpine exposure and maximize available light.

LEFT: The sea urchin pine (Pinus strobus 'Sea Urchin') is very even and predictable in growth form and habit. After 5 years in the garden this 10-year-old plant is only 12" (30 cm) tall.

RIGHT: Small, round, flat river pebbles along an edge create a fabulous rock feature. The garden has a formal feel with individual parts symmetrically placed around a central axis point.

Symmetry is achieved in an informal garden when the different elements on two sides of a central axis point are equal. The plant pot in this garden acts as a fulcrum while the hosta on the left balances the weight of the dwarf blue spruce on the right. (DESIGN BY MARK RUSSELL)

Blue star juniper (Juniperus squamata) is appropriate for a formal garden because its growth habit is easily controlled and predictable.

On the prairies, however, gardens receive light that is harsh and intense. Prairie photographers like George Webber recognize the power of prairie light: "It's too hard," claims Webber, "too bright, too big, often too flat, often lacking in subtlety. It's too dry, too clear, too loud, too relentless. Light becomes a real thing, a tangible thing. A physical thing. There's nothing to block it on the prairies." Prairie gardeners share his concern.

Prairie gardens receive a dramatically higher number of sunny hours throughout the year. Environment Canada's 30-year statistics for hours of sunshine can't accurately reflect the differences in light intensity, but they do give an idea of the differences in total hours of prairie sunshine compared to other sites across the country. In Vancouver and Seattle, which have an overall gardening approach and climate

similar to that of Great Britain, gardens receive an average of 1,600 hours of sun per year. Compare this to Canada's sunniest spot—Estevan, Saskatchewan—which receives on average 2,537 hours of sun per year. This means a garden in Estevan receives almost 60 percent more light than a garden in Vancouver, while a garden in Edmonton (on the fringe of the boreal forest so not even officially on the prairie) receives 40 percent more sun than Vancouver. Although many of these sunshine hours are in the winter, when rock garden plants are presumably dormant, the overall differences are still noteworthy because a very westerly site exposed to full wind and light is going to affect plants year round.

You need to ignore conventional gardening book wisdom and orient your garden so it will not dry or burn out too quickly in the season or even within the day. The best sites will be oriented toward the east or northeast instead of the southwest as suggested by British and coastal gardeners unless your garden focuses exclusively on succulent, drought-tolerant plants. You

also may locate a garden beneath the shelter of a larger tree or near a building to provide relief from the intense midday sun and strong drying winds. In my own front yard, a small alpine garden is nestled in an east-facing site with limited south sun. Afternoon shade and shelter from the west are provided by the house.

With practical concerns taken care of, you'll want to consider the aesthetic potential of your location. Is the rock garden, for example, to be a major feature of your garden and constructed on a grand scale, or will it be a smaller area tucked

TOP: Dianthus alpinus *(a dwarf rock garden pink) is an excellent mounding plant for nestling between rocks in a berm garden. These pinks require a half- to full-sun position.* (ILLUSTRATION BY KATHERINE VINISH)

BOTTOM: The fern leaf bleeding heart (Dicentra eximia) is a long-blooming delicately textured addition to the shady rock garden.

*CONIFER
COMPARISON
CHART (10-YEAR
GROWTH):*
*1. Creeping blue
globe spruce*
(Picea pungens
var. glauca
'Procumbens')
*2. Little giant
cedar* (Thuja
occidentalis 'Little
Giant')
3. Nest spruce
(Picea abies
'Nidiformis')
*4. Columnar blue
spruce* (Picea
pungens var.
glauca 'Fastigiata')
*5. Colorado blue
spruce* (Picea
pungens)
*6. Dwarf globe
blue spruce*
(Picea pungens
'Glauca Globosa')
*7. Dwarf Norway
spruce* (Picea
abies 'Pumila')
8. Mugo pine
(Pinus mugo)
*9. Bristlecone
pine* (Pinus
aristata)
*10. Dwarf slow-
mound mugo pine*
(Pinus mugo
pumilio
'Slowmound')
*11. Ohlendorf
spruce* (picea abies
'Ohlendorffii')
(ILLUSTRATION BY
KATHERINE VINISH)

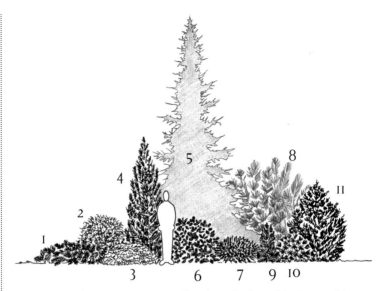

into a corner that invites a sense of discovery? Will the site be viewed from all sides or will it abut a fence or other structure that will limit viewing? Would the addition of a winding stone path invite closer inspection?

Consider, as well, whether the site is to be viewed from your home or simply from the garden itself once you are outside. If the site is currently not visible from the home, would building up the site allow you to enjoy it from inside your home? If there are very few evergreens in your yard, would a woody backdrop of dwarf conifers enhance the planting? Obviously, full-sized spruce will become too large if used as a rock garden backdrop, but a layering of dwarf forms will give depth and interest to the landscape without becoming a long-term liability.

Perhaps the only site to avoid putting a rock garden is dead center in your yard, which has been aptly described as a "dog's grave" because it has no reference to the rest of your landscape.

Basic Elements of Design

After visiting nature and deciding what kind of scene will inspire the look of your rock garden, you are ready to begin designing it. Whether you recognized it or not, what made your chosen scene attractive is that it possessed certain inherent qualities that provoked a sense of beauty. If you wanted to break this scene down, you would discover that it was governed by eight principles of design: line, form, texture, color, repetition, variety, balance and emphasis.

Line

Perhaps the single most important design consideration in any landscape—but especially in the rock garden—is the careful use of line. Nothing creates chaos in design like the lack of strong line. Even a random mix of plants will be unified when the rock garden outline is clear and defined.

This basic outline may be emphasized either with clear edging around the garden or with outline materials such as a small rock wall, a sidewalk, a narrow defined path of turf or other edging material. The outline may be composed of straight edges or curved beds—it makes no difference as long as it is consistent.

The outline of the garden also may be emphasized with the consistent use of rocks in alignment throughout the garden. Aligned rocks will not necessarily be in tidy rows, but they will make geological sense. This often means the strata within the rock create a consistent pattern throughout the garden, or the rocks are aligned along a sloping face and tilt back into the hill at the same angle.

As with all good design, the strong use of line in a rock garden gives sense to the composition, outlines areas and draws attention to special features. Where a particularly strong focal point is desired, it is a good idea to have an intersection of lines—for instance, a single line of rock splitting to form two lines. The eye naturally follows these lines, and their intersections are the best place to use a brilliant flower or a dynamic changing plant such as a shrub with dramatic fall or spring color.

Form

Form extends the principle of line first to the overall shape of the garden and second to the outline of the various plants and rocks used. The principle of form advocates gardens that are long, rectangular and formal or softly curved and informal, instead of irregular forms composed of tight squiggles, dips and dives.

Plants within the garden also will have one of a variety of forms, generally including mounding, mounding foliage with upright flowers, ground covers, upright or loose. Rocks within the garden may be slablike, blocky and square, or softly rounded. Using the principle of form, you can

A fabulous line is created by the low rock wall curving its way through Sheila Paulson's backyard alpine garden.

Scattered rocks set in irregular fashion create confusion. A well-designed rockery will have clear lines and a point of emphasis.

A strong sense of line is felt when manmade elements (pool and path) follow the same general form as the outline of the rock garden seen here in Jackie Dean's garden.

The principle of line is illustrated everywhere in a good garden such as the Paulson's. Line is seen in the raised rock-wall beds, the fence, the bricks and even in the shadows falling in the path.

make design decisions that harmonize these elements. A small outcrop of rock, for instance, may have straight lines that create a triangular form, which may be repeated in an individual dwarf evergreen such as an Ohlendorf spruce *(Picea abies* 'Ohlendorffii'). Conversely, a round smooth fieldstone may call for a globe-shaped plant. In other cases flat and slablike rocks inspire the use of flat ground covers.

The important thing to know about form is that consistency leads to continuity and simplicity. Mix and match various forms—straight edges against curved or round rocks against blocky only within your comfort level.

Texture

Plants come in various textures but can be generally categorized as fine, medium or coarse. Rocks also have textures derived from their size, color and overall appearance. Rock gardens need texture from plants or from the contrast between plants and rocks to create variety and interest. If every plant is of the same fine, medium or coarse texture in a landscape, the finished effect is bland.

Finely textured plants have very narrow leaves or an overall small stature. Good choices for the rock garden include blue star juniper *(Juniperus squamata* 'Blue Star'), any of the small dianthus *(Dianthus* spp.), mother of thyme *(Thymus serpyllum)*, blue-eyed grass *(Sisyrinchium montanum)*, and the delicate low-growing veronicas *(Veronica armena, Veronica prostrata* and *Veronica whitelyii).*

Medium textures include plants such as perennial geranium *(Geranium cinereum)*, native coral bells *(Heuchera cylindrica)* and hybrid

LEFT: Dianthus (Dianthus microlepsis) and river rock share the same form in Margaret Brown's garden.

RIGHT: Silver mound (Artemisia schmidtiana 'Silver Mound') is fairly flat by the end of the season, and its form repeats the appearance of the flat sandstone. Meanwhile the silver leaves of the Red Fox Veronica (Veronica cv. Red Fox) repeat the same foliage color as the silver mound.

coral bells *(Heuchera* cvs.), lady's mantle *(Alchemilla alpina)* and parts of plants such as the pine needle clumps of *Pinus mugo* 'Mops'.

Coarse textures are harder to find in rock garden plants. Bergenia *(Bergenia cordifolia)*, or leatherleaf as it is also called, is suited to both shady and sunny sites. The dwarf globe blue spruce *(Picea pungens*

cvs.) may also be considered coarse if the whole plant is evaluated, and the prickly pear cactus *(Opuntia* spp.) has very broad flat pads instead of leaves, giving it a coarse appearance.

Texture in the rock also may be provided by the finish of the leaves. A fuzzy-leaved lamb's ear *(Stachys byzantia)* definitely has a coarser texture than a shiny-leaved Gentian *(Gentiana* spp.) even if the leaves themselves are about the same size. Unlike gentians, lamb's ears' fuzzy leaves beg to be felt. This tactile feature adds texture beyond its leaves, which contrast the many smaller-leaved rockery plants such as dianthus *(Dianthus* spp.) and draba *(Draba* spp.). Other leaves with touchable texture include the large waxy leatherleaf *(Bergenia cordifolia)*, the satiny round-leaved coral bell *(Heuchera* spp. and cvs.), the almost rubbery auricula primula *(Primula auricula)* and the many

succulent and waxy leaves of the sedums *(Sedum* spp.), saxifrages *(Saxifraga* spp.) and sempervivums *(Sempervivium* spp.).

The choice of mulch makes an additional textural statement in the rock garden. A very fine grit or pea gravel will add fine texture while sharp-edged rock mulch will add a coarser texture. Similarly, rocks used flat on the ground provide a softer finer texture than rocks installed at sharp angles.

I once saw a photo that illustrated a way to test a garden's level of textural interest. The garden was photographed in black and white (you could also make a black and white photocopy of a color photo). While color photos draw the eye to spots of color throughout a scene, a black and white image will allow a critical analysis of the textural interest in the view presented. Ideally, a garden will be texturally varied throughout, and this texture will appear most clearly in the black and white image.

To achieve a garden with good textural contrast, choose rocks larger than 12" (30 cm) on any single dimension. These will look coarser than smaller rocks, whose texture is similar to many fine-textured rock garden plants.

A garden can be analyzed for textural interest by transforming a color photo to black and white. Here strong color contrast belies a lack of texture that is evident when the scene is viewed in black and white.

Color

The impact of color on human response has been studied widely in the fine arts, and in the clothing and interior design industries. Landscapers largely borrow from the other arts to get a fresh look and an effective and pleasing blend of tones in the garden. Chic and trendy color combinations are easiest to achieve in annual flower gardens and flower pots because new colors of annuals are released each year to meet the changing desires of gardeners. Plants that used to come in one or two shades, such as the annual flowering tobacco *(Nicotiana* cvs.), now come in lime and salmon as well as pink, red and white.

With perennials, however, there isn't as much fashionable breeding for color, and this is especially true of those plants used in rock gardens. The obsession among rock gardeners is directed more toward breeding smaller, many-flowered or longer-blooming plants than toward breeding new blossom colors.

Rock garden plants have interesting leaf and flower colors naturally. The most vibrant blues to be found in the plant world, for instance, come from the many rock garden gentians *(Gentiana* spp.); the brightest pinks are in the dwarf Douglasias *(Douglasia montana)* and dianthus *(Dianthus* spp.). The leaves of the many hens and chicks *(Sempervivums* spp. and *Jovibarba* spp.) are colored red or dark maroon while several other plants have white or yellow variegated leaves or are available in silver or blue tones. If the leaf colors of the plants chosen add some variety to the landscape, and especially if some of the color is seasonal or changing, the garden will always have a dynamic look about it and will be an interesting place to visit at any time of year.

The brilliant purple flowers of this Aster alpinus *cultivar bring a spot of intense color to the corner of the garden in late May.*

In a shade corner with very little direct light and almost no hope of color through blooms, the variegated leaf of lungwort (Pulmonaria cv.) *contrasts well with the texture and light green color of sweet woodruff* (Galium odoratum).
(GARDEN BY SHIRLEY SCOTT)

Spots of color from rock garden flowers, leaves and rocks are unlike color in any other garden. Big showy splashes of color typical of perennial borders require careful consideration of the color wheel. In the rock garden, however, color is more pointed and isolated. This allows you to choose a colorful rock you like, select a color of mulch that works with your rock and then simply pick the plants you prefer. There is no need to consult fashion or color theory because the splash of color from an individual rock garden "jewel" does not need to be considered in reference to other plants sharing the rock garden.

Flower color is an accent and bonus and not the primary consid-

Variegated rockcress (Arabis ferdinandi-coburgii 'Variegata') adds immediate interest to the landscape with its brilliantly edged variegated leaves. This low ground cover sports small white flowers for a brief time in June.

eration when choosing plants for the rock garden. Color is in the details—for instance, a bright yellow draba *(Draba* spp.) planted just below a brilliant orange lichen or a dark blue gentian *(Gentiana* spp.) repeated as often as desired to create a shocking moment when it is blooming in May.

Repetition

While it is exciting to have a pleasing variety of forms, textures and colors in the landscape, the overall effect in the garden will be mayhem if every single plant is different. Just as gold earrings are often matched to the gold buttons on a jacket or a fine silk suit is matched to highly polished shoes,

there should be some repetition of elements in the rock garden.

Designers suggest using odd numbers of plants for effective informal repetition. Three, five or seven of the same plant should be bought at the same time. Don't wait until the one plant you buy can be divided into three! These little swaths of form, texture and color naturally draw the eye progressively through the garden.

Color repetition can be achieved, for example, with repeated use of plants with silver leaves. These plants are naturally suited to the bright prairie light and also are usually tolerant of dry conditions. A number of rock plants share this silver leaf trait. Consider silver mound *(Artemisia schmidtiana* 'Silver Mound'), Veronica *(Veronica armena)*, Acantholimon bracteatum, basket of gold alyssum *(Aurinia saxatalis)*, snow-in-summer *(Cerastium tomentosum)*, Dianthus *(Dianthus gratianopolitanus)*, Edelweiss *(Leontopodium alpinum)* and silky scorpion weed *(Phacelia sericea)*.

Repetition should be extended to the color, texture and form of rocks.

Variety

If every plant in the garden has silver leaves, it won't matter how interesting your line is or how often you vary texture and form. The overall effect will be boredom, and the garden will not look personalized or individual. It will look com-

Plants that spill over rocks and walls will soften the look of the rock and create interesting repeating patterns of foliage.

Rocks of similar size and shape are placed in a similar way around a small corner of a garden to enhance repetition of form and color.

Plants and rocks repeat the same form in this unusual garden of small mounding plants and smooth river rock. (GARDEN BY MARGARET BROWN)

Vary texture, color and form to get the ideal blend of interest in the rock garden. In this scene the highest point of interest or emphasis occurs at the intersection of rock and plants, where the spiky coarse background Iris leaves contrast the bright blue leaves of sedum ewersii (Hylotelephium ewersii) *in the middle. Golden Creeping Jenny* (Lysimachia nummularia 'Aurea') *completes the design in front.* (GARDEN BY PETER BRAUN)

mercial and dull. Think of the shopping mall landscapes you may have viewed, where 400 of the same juniper are combined with a repeating red-leaved shrub and single species of deciduous tree. While simplicity is an admired design concept achieved through the tasteful use of repetition, only an advanced designer can successfully create interest when the same plant varieties are repeated too frequently. Even an all-white room in a professional interior design will have contrast in the textures of fabrics and form of furnishings, so new gardeners should take note: repetition is good, but don't repeat a particular form, texture or color so frequently that the garden loses a sense of variety. On the other hand, don't give in to every whim and buy every new plant available or your garden will end up looking chaotic.

The principle of varying texture, color and form within the plants used in the rock garden is difficult to quantify. The goal in a well-

The repetition of rock in a predictable and regular way gives viewers a sense of order and comfort even though a wide variety of plants are employed.

designed garden scene is to achieve balance between too much repetition and too much variety. Also bear in mind that the goal is to provide variety throughout the seasons and the different bloom times of your plant material.

Balance

When the right proportions are reached between repetition and variety of the forms, colors and textures of plants in the garden landscape, it is said to be balanced. Balance does not just mean that groups of matching sentinel junipers *(Juniperus* spp.) are placed in equal quantities on both sides of the front step. It means that the overall mass of plants used on two sides of an imaginary axis is the same and that within the landscape no one item predominates, hogging all the attention.

Think of balance as a teeter totter. If a single plant is dominant on one side of the teeter totter—whether through size, form, color or

Balance is achieved in this scene where the visual weight of rock, evergreen and blooming plants is about equal. From the top left corner the plants are Cembra pine (Pinus cembra) *and little leaf lilac* (Syringa meyeri 'Palibin') *as backdrop to fairies' thimbles* (Campanula cochleariifolia) *and globe blue spruce* (Picea pungens 'Glauca globosa') *in the Paulson garden.*

texture—several smaller plants will need to be placed on the other side to balance it. Bear in mind, too, that darker larger-leaved plants will look coarse and heavy, and may need to be used more sparingly against lighter colors and textures. Remember also that evergreens will dominate the garden during the dormant season, so it is wise to plan a balanced presentation of the species to provide a harmonious winter scene. Gardeners new to rock gardening will be wise to consider a single heavy plant such as a dwarf evergreen pine *(Pinus cembra* cv.) near the central axis point with a larger number of lighter plants moving away from the axis. Finally, don't be afraid to experiment with

In the Shaver–Strelau garden, balance is achieved when the right proportions are reached between repetition and variety of plant and rock forms, colors and textures.

balance during the construction and planting of the garden. Step back from time to time to see if your plan really does produce a sense of balance, and then make changes as appropriate.

A further consideration in achieving balance in the rock garden is the relationship between rocks and plants. The ideal rock garden has a pleasing balance between the two. If, for example, the mature size of the plants you choose will overshadow the rocks, you may need to consider using rocks of larger stature or limiting the maximum allowable size of plants to 12" (30 cm) tall. Because large rocks are difficult to move and large plants are likely to hide small rocks completely, many rock gardeners do keep plants under 12". If very small rocks or rock outcroppings are used, it may be wise to focus on alpine plants or species that will stay compact and under 6" (15 cm) tall. If the landscape and your budget allow rock to be brought in entirely by

When the mass of rock outweighs the mass of plants, it is hard to achieve a balanced look in a garden.

A point of emphasis is created when plants are showcased between a wedge of rock. Stone crop (Sedum acre) is a rather invasive plant and is not recommended, but it is glorious in bloom just above the purple mother-of-thyme (Thymus serpyllum).

crane, you can obviously be more flexible with the size of plants. As a general principle, ensure that the overall visual weight of the plants does not greatly exceed the overall visual weight of the rocks.

Emphasis

A final principle of design is emphasis, both within the larger garden scene and within the rock garden itself. Your rock garden's size, placement and use of color will determine whether your rock garden is the focal point of the entire scene. If, for example, your rock garden is the dominant theme in the landscape, then perhaps consider adding stone paths to lead the eye and invite closer viewing. Within

the rock garden the focal point may be a very interesting plant form, a piece of sculpture or a central grouping of plants with high interest. It is ideal to draw attention to this area by creating dissecting lines of rock or by arranging plants in larger or smaller groups leading to this point.

When all other principles of design are used and a point of emphasis is created in the garden, the overall space is a success. For veteran gardeners the point of emphasis may change with the seasons, but novice gardeners shouldn't push it. This is a level of complexity perhaps too difficult to achieve with a first design. Start instead by designing at least one point of emphasis into the garden— for example, a colorful grouping of plants or a single rock carved out to receive a sparkle of water.

If extremely low maintenance is a goal, choose plants such as the nest spruce *(Picea abies* 'Nidiformis'), which will eventually fill 1 sq yd (1 sq m) with little or no maintenance. Two dozen Lewisia *(Lewisia cotyledon)*, on the other hand, may fill the same area but will require deadheading and frequent replacement due to winterkill. Likewise, one of the small dianthus *(Dianthus microlepsis)* enjoys a long life with rather minimal care, but the glorious longlasting bloom of the Fairies' thimbles *(Campanula cochleariifolia)* may require more maintenance but may prove worth the extra effort for a visually exciting point of emphasis.

This tiny window garden is meant to be viewed from a basement-level window so that the miniature plants can be seen at eye level from inside the home. (PHOTO AND GARDEN BY JOEY STEWART)

CHAPTER 2

Selecting Plants for the Rock Garden

P RAIRIE GARDENERS HAVE BEEN known to complain that the harsh western climate limits choices for perennial gardens. But this is not a complaint to be heard from prairie rock gardeners, who can choose from a broad variety of perennial plants suitable for Zones 1 to 5 and a growing list of woody plants, both deciduous and evergreen.

The plant list at the end of this chapter contains over 200 varieties of plants that will thrive in prairie rock gardens. For each species mentioned, many more cultivars are available and even more are being developed by home gardening enthusiasts and nurseries or are being discovered in mountainous and northern regions around the globe. Well-known plants such as *Sedum kamtschaticum*, for example, originally came from the

A tiny species tulip emerges in May from a glorious carpet of stemless Gentian (Gentiana acaulis), creating an exciting burst of spring color in the rock garden.
(PHOTO BY BILL QUAYLE)

51

Kamchatka Peninsula just off the Bering Sea, a region now being explored for its hardy woody plants. As rockery plants are brought into wider cultivation and as dwarf arctic species are recognized as valuable rock garden additions, the list will continue to grow.

Though the plants in the list are all considered hardy for the prairies, you should consult the following zone maps to check your growing zone. The prairie zones, based on average annual minimum temperatures, range from zero to five and are further subdivided. Remember, however, that climatic zones are guidelines only. Mountain areas, for example, can extend from Zone 1 in high alpine environments to Zone 5 on the lower western slopes. Away from the mountains, the true prairie flatlands are, on average, Zone 3, but some regions such as southern Alberta may be as warm as Zone 4.

Climatic zone variations will also occur within the microclimates of your landscape. For example, the side of your house exposed to cold prevailing winds could be Zone 2 while the sheltered sunny side could be Zone 4. Nevertheless, as a general rule you can feel confident trying any of the rock garden plants listed at the end of this chapter, but you may need to be more diligent in maintaining those listed as hardy in Zones 4 and 5. Plants such as the low-growing rosyveil Peter Pan

group of saxifrages (such as *Saxifraga* cv. 'Rozenzwerg'), for example, are not always listed for Zones 2 to 4 but will often survive several years on the prairies because our dry climate generally prevents the condition of standing water that causes the crowns to rot.

Zone maps are a useful starting point but always bear in mind that plant ratings may vary widely depending upon who defined their hardiness. For example, extremely hardy plants such as columbine *(Aquilegia* spp.) included in the plant list are noted in the *Index of Garden Plants* as hardy from zones 2 to 8, when they are actually hardy to zones 2 through 3 because they survive and even thrive on the prairies.

With your growing zone identified and a clear idea of your location's microclimate, you can begin to look at plant selection more aesthetically. While you may want the full effect of a mature rock garden in its first season, resist the temptation to overplant. It is better to let the plants grow into the garden rather than be obliged to remove or cut back fast growers within a year or two. Remember, too, that no matter how long you garden there will always be a new plant discovery, and it's nice to have a place to put new acquisitions as you find them rather than always having to renovate or extend the garden.

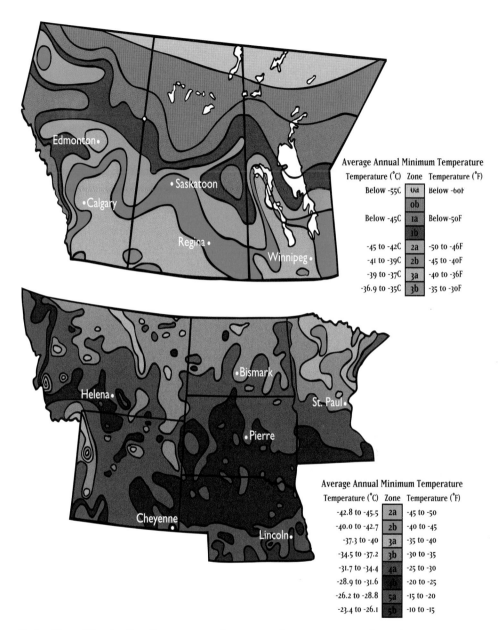

Average Annual Minimum Temperature

Temperature (°C)	Zone	Temperature (°F)
Below -55C	0a	Below -60F
	0b	
Below -45C	1a	Below-50F
	1b	
-45 to -42C	2a	-50 to -46F
-41 to -39C	2b	-45 to -40F
-39 to -37C	3a	-40 to -36F
-36.9 to -35C	3b	-35 to -30F

Average Annual Minimum Temperature

Temperature (°C)	Zone	Temperature (°F)
-42.8 to -45.5	2a	-45 to -50
-40.0 to -42.7	2b	-40 to -45
-37.3 to -40	3a	-35 to -40
-34.5 to -37.2	3b	-30 to -35
-31.7 to -34.4	4a	-25 to -30
-28.9 to -31.6	4b	-20 to -25
-26.2 to -28.8	5a	-15 to -20
-23.4 to -26.1	5b	-10 to -15

Selecting Plants for Four-Season Interest

Growing seasons are short on the prairies, and it seems a shame not to extend the garden's appeal into the winter months. This is especially true for prairie rock gardens, whose appeal comes not just from blooms but from the structure supplied by rocks and woody plants.

I often suggest that at least 50 percent of the planting area be reserved for plants that provide winter interest in a general garden,

Fairies' thimbles are listed in the Index of Garden Plants as a Zone 6 plant, but in reality they are hardy, even aggressive, in Zones 2 and 3 in prairie gardens.

One of the most compact and jewel-like forms of bluebell is the double form, Elizabeth Oliver fairies' thimbles (Campanula cochleariifolia 'Elizabeth Oliver'). This little gem is listed as a Zone 6 plant but has thrived in an open south-facing Calgary garden as surely as any Zone 2 plant. Small rooted cuttings may be lifted from the edge of the mother plant to propagate and share among friends.

choose the remaining 20 percent of the plants for spring and summer glory. Among these, try to choose those that fill two niches: ones that bloom in spring as well as supply off-season texture or interest. These are bonus plants. Hens and chicks *(Sempervivum* cvs.), most sedums *(Sedum* cvs.) and even some dianthus *(Dianthus* spp.), for example, provide a glorious spurt of color in their bloom season but also are evergreen all winter.

Woody Plants

and this guideline applies to the prairie rockery, which is often free of snow while dormant. Any less than this and the garden will be dominated by dead plants and gravel for up to eight months. With 30 percent of the area covered in rock and up to 50 percent in evergreens and other plants with year-round interest, it is a joy to carefully

There is much debate among rock gardeners about whether any woody plants should be included in a rock garden setting. Evergreen conifers send out shallow wide-spreading roots, so some gardeners worry about including them in the garden. If this is a concern, the evergreens can be confined or root pruned as if they are in an outdoor bonsai garden

One of the many delicate dianthus—also known as pinks (Dianthus spp.) has a fine leaf texture that complements the fine rock mulch.

In addition to the year-round effect created by their showy leaves, hens and chicks send up tall flower spikes in midsummer.

instead of a rock garden. This practice, however, may add extra stress to a plant that already has a hard enough time surviving on the prairies, and you may face the prospect of more frequent replacement. Rock gardeners who don't include conifers in their gardens have to make do with the many rock garden plants that stay green over winter. They are usually so low-growing, however, that they do not add much to the overall structure and form to the winter garden because they are often hidden by snow.

I can only imagine how dull a prairie garden space would be if it were confined to plants that die back to the ground in the autumn, so I definitely include woody plants in my rock garden. Woody plants provide four-season interest, and, unlike most perennials, they add height, scale and variety of form to the overall rock garden design.

Two main groups of woody plants are recognized around the world. The first group, the deciduous woody plants, lose their leaves in the autumn. The second, the conifers (sometimes called evergreens), keep most of their leaves in the winter. If evergreens produce cones (even modified cones), they are also known as conifers. Many

One of the rock garden–sized forms of Norway spruce is Picea abies 'Mucronata.' It is less than 24" (60 cm) tall after 10 years of growth. All evergreens add an extra dimension to the rock garden during the winter.

beginners call every cone-producing conifer a pine or fir, but of course these names apply to only a few of the hardy evergreens worth growing here and leave out our biggest hardy group of conifers, the spruce.

Among the woody plants that can be grown successfully on the prairies are the many hardy dwarf cultivars of Norway spruce *(Picea abies* cvs.). These include the lovely *Picea abies* 'Mucronata' and *Picea abies* 'Pumila,' two mounded dwarf Norway spruce with short, dark green needles. Their bright orange winter buds make them especially appealing in the winter garden.

Another excellent choice is *Picea abies* 'Nidiformis,' commonly known as the nest spruce because of its concave mound shape. *Picea abies* 'Ohlendorffii' is a conical, short-needled and compact form of the Norway spruce. When purchased as

a 3' (1-m) -tall shaped and pruned specimen, it may already be 10 years old. After 20 years in the garden it may reach a maximum height of 15' (5 m). Smaller unpruned plants will need to be shaped in the first several years of growing.

Varieties of the dwarf blue spruce include *Picea pungens* 'Iseli Fastigiate,' a columnar form that is usually grafted onto the Norway spruce *(Picea abies).* This narrow spruce has a tight form and uniform blue color. Though seemingly unbothered by extreme exposure to sunlight, it may suffer from snow-load damage, necessitating an occasional trip outdoors to remove snow from its boughs.

Picea pungens glauca 'Procumbens' is a sprawling ground cover form of the blue spruce. It is very blue year round and is a great ground cover for the rock garden or for spilling over a rock wall.

Picea pungens glauca 'St. Mary's Broom' is probably the smallest blue spruce available, although *Picea pungens* 'Thuem' also is a tiny rock garden blue spruce. Both are very hardy, have a compact flat-mounded shape (not rounded) and are uniformly blue.

Pinus aristata 'Sherwood Compact' is a dwarf form of the already small bristlecone pine. Because some bristlecone pines are subject to sunscald, it is wise to place this expensive and special

One of the many native Rocky Mountain dwarf willows (Salix arctica) *sprawls along between rocks, offering its texturally interesting, deeply veined glossy leaves for contrast.*

form in a location with midday or afternoon shade.

Pinus strobus 'Sea Urchin' is a dwarf form of the five-needled Easter white pine *(Pinus strobus)*. This small soft-mounded plant has very tight growth and may need spring cleaning, a task that involves gently tugging the old needles out of the very tight plant mound by hand. Simply comb the loose needles from this shrub with your fingers.

Many excellent dwarf deciduous (nonevergreen) trees and shrubs have made their way into the marketplace and our prairie gardens. Dwarf cotoneasters *(Cotoneaster horizontalis* var. *perpusillus)*, dwarf willow *(Salix* spp.) and dwarf birch *(Betula* spp.) are favorites of prairie rock gardeners. Dwarf cotoneasters are grown almost entirely for their spraylike form, which is much like a juniper's, and for their brilliant red

fall color. Birch, especially the 'Trost dwarf' *(Betula pendula* 'Trost Dwarf' cv.), are grown for their exotic look, which is possibly the closest a prairie hardy plant can come to a Japanese maple in appearance. Dwarf native forms of birch have delicate foliage, which turns brilliant yellow in autumn. Dwarf willows, especially the shiny-leaved native alpine forms, are just entering the market and may be hard to find, but they are definitely worth looking for. Their striking red bark adds winter interest. Look for cultivars or the species *Salix vestita, Salix glauca* and *Salix arctica.*

Selecting Plants for Height

"What follows are only the plants designated as 12" (30 cm) and under and 'appropriate to the rock garden,'" begins the Denver Botanic Gardens database manager Michael Ebbs in his "Rock Garden Plants

The chunky coarse texture of the dwarf globe blue spruce (Picea pungens 'Glauca globosa') is an asset in any garden, but because of its bright blue color this high graft form is especially useful in the winter rock garden.

approximates the lean soils found in nature.

Mature plant height may also be restricted by choosing specially selected cultivars. The common shasta daisy *(Leucanthemum x superbum)*, for instance, hardly seems like a rock garden plant because it gets so long and leggy—up to 30" (75 cm) tall—in the dappled shade of most well-established gardens. However, the extremely compact cultivar *Leucanthemum x superbum* 'Snow Lady' works nicely in the rock garden because it usually grows no taller than 12" (30 cm).

Be aware that species plants (sometimes known as native plants) grown from seed will have more genetic variability than cultivars. Species plants are usually variable because they have a wide genetic base and have not usually been "selected," a process of breeding or choosing plants for special features such as shorter stems or abundant flowers. Cultivars, on the other hand, *are* bred for specific variations, and among them you may find more compact versions of species plants.

Selecting Plants for Form

Occasionally, plant forms are manipulated by gardeners to create artificial shapes such as poodle-trimmed junipers or lollipop-shaped trees. But the vast majority of rock garden plants are not tampered with in this manner, so plants' nat-

Beginner's List" from a North American Rock Garden Society quarterly bulletin. As Michael Ebbs knows, height is the most critical characteristic to consider when selecting plants for the rock garden because the essence of rock gardening is the combination of rock and plant. If one of these greatly overshadows the other, the very basis of good rock garden design is lost.

In almost every climate the height of a plant, however, is determined not only by its genetics but also by soils. It often happens that a plant known to be low-growing in its natural environment, due to the harshness of the climate or lean condition of the soil, will surprise gardeners with its mature size in well-watered, rich garden soil. Some of this variation can be minimized by blending special rock garden soil for your garden *(see pages 141–43 for soil mixes)* that better

ural forms become an important consideration when selecting specimens to suit your rock garden's overall design.

The plant list at the end of this chapter identifies basic plant forms to help new gardeners understand the natural form of the plants. These forms include mounding, tight-mounding (or bun-shaped), mounding foliage with upright flowers, ground covers, uprights, and loose (or trailing). Each plant form adds a distinct shape to the rock garden, so all types should be considered.

Mounding and Tight-Mounding Forms

Mounding and tight-mounding plants include all those with an overall spherical shape such as blue fescue *(Festuca glauca* cvs.) and perennial pinks *(Dianthus* spp. or cvs.). Most mounding plants in the rock garden are easy to work with.

They fill a defined area and cover the ground completely beneath them. The mounding form may be accentuated in alpine plants, which become extremely tight and compact. This form has been described as tight-mounding, or bun-shaped, and plants with this shape make extremely compact and almost rigid globes in the garden. Blooms on this form are an extra treat.

Some of my favorite mounding and tight-mounding forms include draba *(Draba* spp.), whose yellow blooms appear so suddenly in early spring that they often become one of the season's first delights.

Primulas (such as *Primula hirsuta)* are a great mounding plant for the rock garden. They may look dainty, but they are very hardy even in dry conditions in full sun, and their pink flowers hover just above sensuous fleshy leaves.

Blue clips bellflowers *(Campanula*

LEFT: Plants take on a new shape and look during the first winter snow. Here, blue fescue (Festuca glauca) *is at a high point in late fall before its blue color fades completely.*

RIGHT: Draba's (Draba spp.) *tight-mounding form and reliable brilliant yellow color in early spring make it a valuable addition to the prairie rock garden.*

Mounding Foliage with Upright Flowers

This variation of the mounding or tight-mounding form includes plants whose profile changes with the season. Typically, they produce leaves that grow in a uniform mound, but they also produce upright flower stalks that emerge from the middle of the mound to give them a different form during the blooming season.

Some mounding plants with upright flowers that make ideal additions to the prairie rock garden include coral bells *(Heuchera* cvs.), which are grown for their interesting green, speckled white or very dark burgundy foliage as much as for their delicate flowers that bloom in shades of pink or creamy white.

Alpine rockfoil *(Saxifraga cotyledon)* is another good choice. It tolerates full sun, and clusters of large white flowers on 20" (50-cm) stems emerge in late spring, spilling over the foliage almost completely.

Lewisias *(Lewisia cotyledon)* come in an amazing variety of colors from pale yellow to neon pink and flourescent orange, which makes them showy additions to virtually any rock garden. Be careful to plant them on an angle or in rock crevices so rain doesn't sit directly in their center crown, which will cause it to rot.

In the shade rock garden, try Cortusoides primula *(Primula cortusoides)*, which provides excite-

The leaves of native coral bells (Heuchera cylindrica) contrast amazingly well with the fine gravel mulch beneath them. Because the leaves, rather than the flowers, are the key feature of this plant, it provides many months of interest in the prairie rock garden. (GARDEN BY DONNA BALZER)

carpatica 'Blue Clips') are a rock garden favorite because their tight-mounding dark green leaves sport a carpet of blue bellflowers from early to late summer.

Blue fescue *(Festuca glauca* cvs.) is one of many ornamental grasses suitable for rock gardens. Its blue leaves and mounding form add a very distinctive texture to the garden. As a bonus it also tolerates intense heat and drought. For shadier spots, mounding plants include auricula primulas *(Primula auricula)*, which offers an early splash of color ranging from yellow to purple, and yellow corydalis *(Corydalis lutea)*, a member of the poppy family that offers gorgeous yellow blooms all season.

ment with broad leaves that dramatically contrast a tall spike of pink flowers.

Ground Cover Forms

Ground covers tend to creep over and completely fill the ground between rocks, even growing over rocks they encounter. They may be annuals, perennials or woodies, and though interest often comes solely from their form, texture or leaf color, many of them bloom as well.

Some blooming ground covers worthy of consideration in the rock garden include mountain avens *(Dryas octopetala)*, a woody plant with large creamy flowers that grow to 1" (2.5 cm) across in early summer. It's suited to dry rock gardens in even the harshest climate. Although it may become widespread once established, it should definitely rank high on the rock garden ground-cover list.

Pussytoes *(Antennaria rosea)* are a tight ground cover found in both prairie and mountain conditions. They creep compactly between flagstone or narrow rock cracks, and their soft, grey, feltlike leaves cling to the soil. Flowers emerge from the leaves but are not overly showy.

Creeping Jenny *(Lysimachia nummularia)* is one of the most effective ground covers for contrast with rock color in shady areas. This dwarf plant grows very tight to the ground as it creeps around and spills over rocks. The golden-leaved cultivar *Lysimachia nummularia* 'Aurea' is especially showy in shade.

Saxifrages such as the widely available Peter Pan or mossy saxifrages *(Saxifraga* cvs.) make a fine green carpet in a neatly spreading circle. When in bloom these plants take center stage with their large, showy white or pink flowers.

Stemless gentian *(Gentian acaulis)*

LEFT: Spring gentian (Gentiana verna), like its larger cousin the stemless gentian (Gentian acaulis), is a brilliant blue beacon in the late spring garden.

RIGHT: The early summer blooms of the various saxifrage cultivars (Saxifraga x arendsii) range from pure white to soft pink and deep brilliant pink, but as a group these plants are short-lived in the garden.

LEFT: Moss campion (Silene acaulis) is brilliantly pink and simultaneously in bloom across the plant in its native mountain habitat, but the flowers are more sporadic in cultivation.

RIGHT: Creeping speedwell (Veronica prostrata) is a reliable ground cover with its glossy green leaves and brilliant, late spring, blue or pink blooms.

and spring gentian *(Gentian verna)* are probably the most brilliantly blue prairie hardy ground covers available. They are also reliably evergreen even in the Chinook zone. Stemless gentians are 1" (2.5-cm) tall with showy 1.5" (4-cm) -long blue trumpets that appear in late May. The spring gentians are under 1" (2.5 cm) tall with equally bright blue blooms.

Moss campion *(Silene acaulis)* is a Rocky Mountain native creeping ground cover whose flat pink flowers rest directly on the foliage. While these spring simultaneously and completely into a carpet of bloom in their mountain habitat, they often sport only a sprinkling of color in the late spring and summer garden.

Ground cover veronicas *(Veronica* spp.), also known as speedwell, are wonderfully drought tolerant and bloom in early summer. Many have grey leaves, and all have either blue or pink blossoms individually or

clustered on short stems. Check the names listed on page 129 or check plant labels to ensure you are getting dwarf, not tall, forms.

The flower stalks of bergenia *(Bergenia* spp.) can reach a height of 18" (45 cm), which typically restricts their use to larger rock gardens, but their coarse leaves make them appealing if distinctive texture is desired. Bergenias also are a good choice because they adapt to both dry and moist environments in shade and full sun.

Upright Forms

Anyone who has ever used a draceana in the center of a pot full of geraniums knows the value of an upright plant in any garden setting. Although our choices in the rock garden are limited to a few penstemons, irises and grasses, a planting of well-placed uprights can provide striking contrast to a group of

mounding plants, create transitions between ground covers and taller woody plants, and serve as a stunning focal point.

Suitable upright flowering plants for the larger rock garden include Siberian irises *(Iris sibirica)*, which grow to 3' (90 cm) and sport blue-violet blooms in early summer. Make sure to look for small cultivars when shopping. Smaller spaces will benefit from the inclusion of the smaller *Iris cristata*, which reaches 6–8" (15–20 cm) in height. The dwarf cultivars of *Iris reticulata* and the hybrids between *Iris reticulata* and *Iris histrioides* reach only 4" (10 cm) in height, but their distinctive spiky texture and dark blue to purple blooms are striking and memorable. Some of the cultivars and hybrids of the *Iris reticulata* include the 4" (10-cm) -tall cultivars such as 'Catab,' 'Gordon,' 'Joyce,' 'Natascha' and 'Springtime.' If these dwarf iris-es are allowed to spread over a large area instead of being confined between rocks, they eventually give the effect of a ground cover.

Larger upright forms can be provided by woody plants such as the columnar blue spruce *(Picea pungens* 'Iseli Fastigiate'), which has become justly popular in a wide range of gardens including larger rock gardens. It grows to 16' (5 m) tall and 3' (1 m) wide, is extremely blue and very hardy across the prairies.

The Ohlendorf spruce *(Picea abies* 'Ohlendorffii') is a mid- to dark green hardy evergreen. Its distinctly upright triangular form provides a strong sense of line year-round, but especially in the rock garden in winter.

Loose Forms

Plants that spread or spill rather than form tight mats or mounds are described as loose or even trailing if they have a rock to splash over.

LEFT: Tiny Iris histrioides *'George' may be short-lived on the prairies, but its surprisingly intense dark purple flowers pop out as quickly as the snow melts.*

RIGHT: The tall *gentian (Gentiana septemfida) blooms in late August or early September. It is very lime-sensitive, and it is necessary to acidify the soil around its roots with peat or a similar acidic component to at least neutralize the soil.*

A large clump of fall gentian (Gentiana septemfida) *illustrates the plant's naturally floppy form, which makes it ideal for use at the top of a rock wall or between rocks, where it won't be a disappointment when it sprawls naturally.*
(GARDEN BY DONNA BALZER)

Loose plants add an effective contrast to mounding upright forms and ground cover plants.

Basket of gold alyssum *(Aurinia saxatalis)* is stunning at the top of rock walls as its grey-green leaves spill over the side and its profuse late-spring yellow blooms sway in the breeze. It also thrives in the poor soil in rock cracks and crevices.

Gentians such as *Gentiana kesselringii* produce an abundance of small white blooms in late summer as long as they receive dappled to half sun. Their lower leaves are straplike and broad.

Fall gentians *(Gentiana septemfida)* are aptly named for their late-blooming 2" (5-cm) clusters of blue flowers that appear in late August or early September, adding a last burst of color in the rock garden.

Selecting Plants for Color

Once you have selected woody plants to add structure and four-season interest to the garden, choose plants to supply leaf and

These two cultivars of the pasque flower (introduced from Europe) look a lot like our native prairie crocus. The Pulsatilla vulgaris (formerly Anemone vulgaris) comes in a range of shades from palest purple to dark wine purple. It offers interesting fluffy seed pods for extra attraction after the one- to two-month blooming period.

With its leaves alone, Sedum ewersii (Hylotelephium ewersii)—also known as blue sedum—provides amazing texture and interest, but its bright pink flowers are also a treat in late summer.

bloom color throughout the growing season. Rock garden leaf color ranges from the golden yellow of golden creeping Jenny *(Lysimachia nummularia* "Aurea") to the dark green of thyme *(Thymus serpyllum),* the burgundy of palace purple coral bells *(Heuchera micrantha* "Palace Purple"), the blues of blue sedums *(Hylotelephium ewersii)* and the silver of snow-in-summer *(Cerastium tomentosum).*

Other rock garden plants that add the dimension of silver or silvery blue leaf color are lamb's ears *(Stachys lanata),* veronicas *(Veronica* spp.), acantholinum *(Acantholinum* spp.), many dianthus *(Dianthus* spp.), the various artemisias *(Artemisias* spp.), blue fescue *(Festuca* spp.) and

the ornamental onion *(Allium karataviense).*

Some of the sedums *(Sedum* spp.) and hens and chicks *(Sempervivum* spp.) have red, blue or even pink leaf colors, which also add to the beauty of the garden, especially when fewer plants are blooming during midsummer.

A Plant Name Primer

The nomenclature used for plants in the following plant list can appear intimidating at first glance to those new to gardening. Though the process of naming plants can be complex, it does follow some basic principles that will help you understand how plants are classified.

Normal practice calls for the

Latin plant name to be italicized and followed by the "author," the person recognized as having first named the plant. It is not uncommon, however, that more than one Latin name finds its way into popular usage. Sometimes, for example, a plant is independently discovered in more than one place or time, and keen researchers are left to sort out when it was first discovered. Other times, a plant is discovered, named and then later found to have been placed in the wrong species. Therefore the process of plant name review and reclassification is continuous, but to the home gardener changes seem to happen overnight. In reality the naming of plants is part of a very slow process of study and consideration by professional taxonomists worldwide.

If the accepted plant name has changed or if there is no common name for a plant, the Latin name will sometimes be used as the common name. Crocus, for example, is the common name for *Crocus* spp. If a Latin name is used as the common name it is not italicized or capitalized unless it is named for a place or person.

For common names I use the generally accepted lowercase spelling whenever possible (as in black spruce or lamb's ears). If a proper noun precedes the plant name (such as dwarf Alberta spruce, Norway spruce or Ohlendorf spruce), I use a capital to recognize the proper

noun. I have chosen this naming system based on my 10 years of work as the Calgary Zoo Botanical Garden horticulturist, where a system was adopted to bring some conformity to the wide range of names used in the garden's database and throughout the plant signage on the grounds. The practice largely conforms to rules followed by other major botanical gardens around the world.

In this book I have tried to use the most current and internationally recognized references available. This most often means *The Index of Garden Plants* (1995) but may include other references, including catalogues if the cultivar is newly introduced to the trade.

Hens and chicks (Sempervivum spp.) come in a range of colors from plain green through to partially maroon through to entirely maroon. They are usually purchased by color and are used throughout the dry sunny prairie garden wherever interesting texture and contrast are needed.

BOTANICAL NAME	COMMON NAME	FAMILY NAME	IDEAL LOCATION (if particular)	HEIGHT
Acantholimon armenum Boiss. & Huet.	n/a	leadwort	open, sunny	2–6" (5–15 cm)
Acantholimon bracteatum (Girard) Boiss.	n/a	leadwort	open, sunny	flowers to 7" (18 cm)
Adonis vernalis L.	spring adonis	buttercup	almost full shade to almost full sun	10–12" (25–30 cm)
Aethionema armenum Boiss.	stone cress	mustard	sunny	6–8" (15–20 cm)
Aethionema oppositifolium (Pers.) Hedge.	stone cress	mustard	sunny; rock cracks	1.5–2" (3–5 cm)
Alchemilla alpina L.	alpine lady's mantle	rose	part shade	6" (15 cm)
Alchemilla conjuncta Bab.	alpine lady's mantle	rose	part shade	6–12"
Alchemilla mollis Rothm.	lady's mantle	rose	part shade to dappled sun	12–18" (30–45 cm)
Allium azureum see *Allium caeruleum* Pall.				

U=UPRIGHT ◆ M=MOUNDING ◆ Gr-C=GROUNDCOVER ◆ L=LOOSE ◆ W=WOODY

FORM	BLOOM COLOR	ESTIMATED BLOOM TIME	COMMENTS
M–B	pink	summer	Originally from Asia Minor, this compact mounding plant with pink flowers is reminiscent of dianthus.
M–B	bright pink	summer	Native to Iran. A very good bun plant.
M	bright yellow	mid- to late May	Very tolerant, fine-textured plant with fragile-looking soft green foliage.
M–U	pink	late spring	Tufted plant with flowers in short racemes (clusters).
Gr-C	soft violet to pink	2–3 weeks early to late April	Leaves are fleshy, blue-green and smooth.
M	soft yellow	late spring to early summer	Lovely mounding plant with leaf segments clearly split to the central leaf blade. The underside of the leaf is silky and hairy.
M	soft yellow	June	Excellent mounding form. Leaves are like *A. alpina*'s, but leaf segments are attached at about the midpoint. Native to stream edges and subalpine meadows, but tolerates a very dry full-sun exposure.
M	soft yellow	late spring to early summer	Loose plant with large hairy leaves. Usually too tall for the small rockery but offers interesting leaf form and texture for the bigger perennial area.

◆ **Tr**=TRAILING ◆ **M–B**=MOUNDING BUN ◆ **M–U**=MOUNDING UPRIGHT

BOTANICAL NAME	COMMON NAME	FAMILY NAME	IDEAL LOCATION (if particular)	HEIGHT
Allium caeruleum Pall.	blue ornamental onion	lily	sunny; moderately moist to dry	8–18" (20–45 cm)
Allium christophii Trautv.	star of Persia	lily	sunny; moderately moist to dry	6–20" (15–50 cm)
Allium karataviense Reg.	n/a	lily	sunny; tolerant of poor soil	4–10" (10–25 cm)
Alyssum saxatile L. see *Aurinia saxatalis*				
Androsace chamaejasme Wulf. in Jacq.	rock jasmine	primula	limestone mountains	1.2–2.5" (3–6 cm)
Androsace lanuginosa. Wallich.	woolly rock jasmine	primula	dappled but bright light; well-drained soil and mulch	1.2–2" (3–5 cm)
Androsace primuloides Duby.	rock jasmine	primula	dappled to half sun; good drainage	2 x 2" (5 x 5 cm) rosettes
Androsace sarmentosa Wallich.	n/a	primula	dappled to half sun; good drainage	2" (5 cm)

U=UPRIGHT ◆ **M**=MOUNDING ◆ **Gr-C**=GROUNDCOVER ◆ **L**=LOOSE ◆ **W**=WOODY

FORM	BLOOM COLOR	ESTIMATED BLOOM TIME	COMMENTS
U	dark blue	June or July	Plant with narrow upright leaves which may multiply slowly in less than favorable conditions. Flowers cluster on narrow stems and offer good color for the midsummer garden. Flower cluster spread approximates 1.2–1.5" (3–4 cm).
L	dusty pink to purple	early summer	This ornamental onion has distinctive blooms in a star-shaped umbel.
M	pale mauve	late spring to early summer	Blooms and seed pods, which both last into the fall, provide interesting substance for the garden. Very coarse texture, unique appearance.
M	creamy white with yellow eye	mid-spring	Compact alpine for tight cracks between rocks. Native to the Rocky Mountains.
M–U	pink to deep purple	late spring to late summer	Trailing plant with narrow, white, hairy leaves and bright flowers.
M–U	pink	May to early June	Nice blooms on ground-hugging silvery rosettes of leaves.
Gr-C	pink	May	Spreads by red stolons, which cascade over rocks. Very showy in new garden. May become invasive but is easily removed if it becomes a problem.

◆ **Tr**=TRAILING ◆ **M—B**=MOUNDING BUN ◆ **M—U**=MOUNDING UPRIGHT

BOTANICAL NAME	COMMON NAME	FAMILY NAME	IDEAL LOCATION (if particular)	HEIGHT
Androsace sempervivoides Jacquem. ex Duby.	n/a	primula	half sun; good drainage	2 x 2" (5 x 5 cm) rosettes
Androsace villosa L.	rock jasmine	primula	part sun	4" (10 cm)
Anemone multifida Poir.	cut-leaved anemone	buttercup	full shade to full sun; dry	6–20" (15–50 cm)
Anemone patens L. *see Pulsatilla patens* (L.) Mill.				
Anemone pulsatilla L. *see Pulsatilla vulgaris* Mill.				
Anemone sylvestris L.	snowdrop windflower	buttercup	dry shade	12" (30 cm)
Antennaria rosea Greene	pussy-toes	daisy	part shade or full sun; dry	leaves to 0.5" (1 cm); 6" (15 cm) in bloom
Aquilegia discolor Levier & Leresche.	columbine	buttercup	part shade	4–6" (10–15 cm)
Aquilegia flabellata var. 'Alba' *pumila* (Huth) Kudo	dwarf white Japanese columbine	buttercup	part shade	8–10" (20–25 cm)

U=UPRIGHT ♦ M=MOUNDING ♦ Gr-C=GROUNDCOVER ♦ L=LOOSE ♦ W=WOODY

FORM	BLOOM COLOR	ESTIMATED BLOOM TIME	COMMENTS
Gr-C	pink	late May to June	Spreads by rosettes. Native to Kashmir.
M—B	pink	June	Intensely silvery and hairy plant. Very compact. Similar in appearance to *A. chamaejasme*. Originally from Europe.
Gr-C to L	white	May to June	Native to prairie grasslands, open woods and forest edges.
Gr-C	white	June	Extremely hardy, perhaps invasive, plant for dry conditions such as the infamous "beneath the spruce tree" location. May want to containerize if used in a mixed rock garden, or use only in the very dry parts. Tolerates sun as well.
Gr-C	white to soft pink	summer	Ideally used in tight spaces between rocks where the silvery color of the leaves can be used to best advantage. Blooms are dry and not showy. Flowers are largely insignificant in comparison to the leaves.
M	blue and cream	early summer	Compact hardy dwarf columbine for mixed garden light.
M	white	May	Compact hardy dwarf plant with clear white blossoms.

◆ **Tr**=TRAILING ◆ **M—B**=MOUNDING BUN ◆ **M—U**=MOUNDING UPRIGHT

BOTANICAL NAME	COMMON NAME	FAMILY NAME		HEIGHT
Aquilegia jonesii Parry.	blue columbine	buttercup	exposed alpine scree	2–8" (5–20 cm)
Aquilegia saximontana Rydb.	columbine	buttercup	alpine areas; scree	4–8" (10–20 cm)
Arabis caucasica Schldl.	rockcress	mustard	full sun; good drainage	up to 8" (20 cm)
Arabis ferdinandi-coburgii 'Variegata' Kellerer & Sunderm.	variegated rockcress	mustard	up to half sun	up to 4" (10 cm)
Armeria caespitosa (Cav) Boiss.	dwarf thrift	leadwort	full sun	up to 6" (15 cm)
Armeria caespitosa 'Bevan's Variety'	Bevan's dwarf thrift	leadwort	up to full sun	up to 2" (5 cm)
Armeria juniperifolia (Vahl) Haffsgg. *see Armeria caespitosa*				
Armeria maritima (Mill) Willd.	common thrift	leadwort	full sun	up to 12" (30 cm)

U=UPRIGHT ◆ M=MOUNDING ◆ **Gr-C**=GROUNDCOVER ◆ **L**=LOOSE ◆ **W**=WOODY

FORM	BLOOM COLOR	ESTIMATED BLOOM TIME	COMMENTS
M	blue	June	Very compact plant from high elevations in southwestern Alberta. May be difficult to get the compact, full-flowering effect in the garden, but it is always worth trying. Even the leaves have a bluish green tone.
M	blue and cream	May to July	Delicate, small-leaved columbine found in high elevations from Utah to Colorado.
Gr-C	usually white	early to late May	Mounding or more often mat-forming plant. Flower stems are loose above the mat of grey leaves and tend to look messy as they mature. Not really a desirable plant, although it is often sold as "similar to" aubretia, which is hardier, more compact and longer blooming.
Gr-C	white	May	Very interesting low-mat plant with variegated leaves. With no snowcover, the plant adds year-round interest to the garden. Leaves are splashed ivory in summer and may take on a pink tinge in fall or winter.
M—B	pink	throughout summer	Small compact tufted plant with a delicate fine-textured look.
M—B	pink	summer	Very compact version of the species.
M	pink	June	Very fine-textured perennial for large sunny rock borders. May die back in dry winters.

◆ **Tr**=TRAILING ◆ **M—B**=MOUNDING BUN ◆ **M—U**=MOUNDING UPRIGHT

BOTANICAL NAME	COMMON NAME	FAMILY NAME	IDEAL LOCATION (if particular)	HEIGHT
Artemisia schmidtiana 'Silver Mound' Maxim.	silver mound	daisy	full sun	up to 18" (45 cm)
Asperula gussonii Boiss.	woodruff	gardenia	shade to part sun; dry to moist	2–4" (5–10 cm)
Aster alpinus L.	alpine aster	daisy	up to full sun; tolerates harsh conditions	up to 12" (30 cm)
Aubrieta x *cultorum* Bergmans. 'Purple Cascade'	purple cascade aubretia	mustard	half to full sun; unsheltered	2" (5 cm)
Aubrieta gracilis Sprun ex Boss	alpine aubretia	mustard	full sun for at least 4 hours	2" (5 cm)
Aurinia saxatalis (L.) Desv.	basket of gold alyssum	mustard	full sun; poor soil or rock cracks	10–12" (25–30 cm)
Bergenia cordifolia (Haw.) Sternb., *B. crassifolia* (L.) Fritsch and *B.* cvs. of mixed parentage	leatherleaf, elephant ears, bergenia	saxifrage	full shade to part sun; dry to part moist	leaves to 12" (30 cm); up to 18" (45 cm) in bloom

U=UPRIGHT ◆ M=MOUNDING ◆ Gr-C=GROUNDCOVER ◆ L=LOOSE ◆ W=WOODY

FORM	BLOOM COLOR	ESTIMATED BLOOM TIME	COMMENTS
M	flowers not significant	n/a	Has very soft, silvery, fine-textured leaves. Excels in very poor soil with a dry sunny aspect. May grow too large for some rock gardens but form and color are excellent in larger spaces.
Gr-C	pink	May	Very fine-textured, low plant which grows between and over rocks.
M	purple	late May and late June or early July	Grows in lax clumps as broad as they are tall. Its intensely purple blossoms have bright yellow centers.
Gr-C	bright purple	May	Leaves form green mats spreading up to 24" (60 cm) a season, sometimes dying back in winter, but usually reseeding nearby. This complex hybrid has many cultivars and includes *A. deltoidea* as a parent.
M–B	bright purple	June	Leaves are sandpaper rough and pale grey-green. Smaller in height and spread than the more common *A.* x *cultorum*. May be hard to find but not difficult to grow from seed. Shortlived if site is too shady.
L, Tr	pale to deep yellow	late May or June	Leaves are grey-green. Flower color intensity varies with the cultivar. After the flowers bloom, the seed pods should be allowed to form and reseed.
Gr-C	pale to dark pink	May	Excellent broad-textured evergreen plant suited to all gardens but especially to difficult dry shade conditions. Blooms appear on narrow stems. Fall foliage is dark burgundy-red.

◆ **Tr**=TRAILING ◆ **M—B**=MOUNDING BUN ◆ **M—U**=MOUNDING UPRIGHT

BOTANICAL NAME	COMMON NAME	FAMILY NAME	IDEAL LOCATION (if particular)	HEIGHT
Betula glandulosa Michx. see *Betula nana* L.				
Betula nana L.	dwarf birch, bog birch, arctic birch	birch	part shade to full sun; boggy, moist	20–79" (50–200 cm)
Betula pendula Roth. 'Trost's Dwarf'	Trost's dwarf birch	birch	half to full sun	20–51" (50–130 cm)
Betula pumila L.	dwarf birch	birch	sunny; boggy, moist	3–10' (1–3 m)
Campanula betulifolia K. Koch.	birchleaf bellflower	bluebell	part shade	4–6" (10–15 cm)
Campanula carpatica Jacq. 'Blue Clips'	blue clips bluebell	bluebell	half to almost full sun	12" (30 cm)
Campanula cochleariifolia Lam.	fairies' thimbles	bluebell	half to full sun	2–4" (4–10 cm)

U=UPRIGHT ◆ M=MOUNDING ◆ Gr-C=GROUNDCOVER ◆ L=LOOSE ◆ W=WOODY

FORM	BLOOM COLOR	ESTIMATED BLOOM TIME	COMMENTS
W	flowers not significant	n/a	Dwarf alpine shrub or small tree with delicate, round, glossy leaves. Fine dark black twigs provide interest in the dormant season. Easy from seed and offers gold autumn color. Native to the Rocky Mountains.
W	flowers not significant	n/a	Delicate and fine-textured small shrub with very finely cut leaves (much like a Japanese maple's). Ideal for the middle or back of sunny rock gardens.
W	flowers not significant	n/a	Small native Rocky Mountain birch with delicate, dark brown branches and glossy green leaves. Easy to grow from seed and offers gold autumn color.
Gr-C	white	mid to late summer	Scrambling, coarse-leaved bellflower best seen trailing between rocks or over walls. Easily started from seed and occasionally invasive. Needs to be monitored.
M	bright blue	throughout summer	Leaves form a tight, bright green mound with blooms popping just above the foliage. 'White Clips' is the same but has bright white blooms. Easily started from seed.
Gr-C	bright blue	from early July	Leaves form a mat or ground cover between and around rocks. Sometimes weedy and difficult to control, but excellent in confined spaces where it can spill between rocks in walls. A very good addition to the July–August garden.

◆ **Tr**=TRAILING ◆ **M—B**=MOUNDING BUN ◆ **M—U**=MOUNDING UPRIGHT

BOTANICAL NAME	COMMON NAME	FAMILY NAME	IDEAL LOCATION (if particular)	HEIGHT
Campanula cochleariifolia Lam. 'Elizabeth Oliver'	double fairies' thimbles	bluebell	dappled to full sun	2–4" (4–10 cm)
Campanula excisa Schleich. ex Murith.	n/a	bluebell	dappled shade to almost full sun	6–8" (15–20 cm)
Campanula lasiocarpa Cham.	harebell	bluebell	dappled to full sun	up to 7" (18 cm)
Campanula portenschlagiana Schult	n/a	bluebell	part shade to almost full sun	4–8" (10–20 cm)
Campanula 'Birch Hybrid'	birch hybrid bluebell	bluebell	part to full sun	6–8" (15–20 cm)
Cerastium tomentosum L.	snow-in-summer	pink	dry shade; poor soil	leaves to 2" (5 cm); 8" (20 cm) in bloom
Chrysanthemum weyrichii see *Dendranthema weyrichii*				
Cortusa mathioli L.	cortusa	primula	shade	12" (30 cm)

U=UPRIGHT ◆ M=MOUNDING ◆ Gr-C=GROUNDCOVER ◆ L=LOOSE ◆ W=WOODY

FORM	BLOOM COLOR	ESTIMATED BLOOM TIME	COMMENTS
Gr–C	pale icy blue	June or July	Creeps slowly to form a wide mat between rocks or a circle if in an open area. Extremely showy in midsummer when leaves can't be seen for weeks because of numerous long-lived blooms. Widely adapted and fully hardy.
U	blue	mid-June	Upright, clump-forming plant with unusually excised petals. May spread by underground roots.
M	blue	early summer	Found in high alpine and arctic tundra conditions as well as rocky outcroppings in the Rocky Mountains.
M	blue	summer	Trailing to somewhat ascending plant for cracks between rocks.
M–Gr-C	light blue	from June	Grows vigorously over walls and between rock cracks. Very long and free flowering.
Gr–C	white	June	Silvery leaves are suited to large, difficult, dry spaces where tree roots or lack of irrigation keep the soil very dry and otherwise inhospitable. A very common plant with a tendency to sprawl. Leaves offer an interesting texture all season.
M–U	pink	June	Looks very similar to primulas with slender flowering stems growing above a foliage mound of softly scalloped leaves. Makes a great transition from the shade garden to the rock garden. Very beautiful.

◆ **Tr**=TRAILING ◆ **M—B**=MOUNDING BUN ◆ **M—U**=MOUNDING UPRIGHT

82

BOTANICAL NAME	COMMON NAME	FAMILY NAME	IDEAL LOCATION (if particular)	HEIGHT
Corydalis lutea (L.) D.C.	yellow corydalis	poppy	shade; moist	12–18" (30–45 cm)
Corydalis 'Blue Panda'	blue panda	poppy	shade; moist	up to 12" (30 cm)
Coryphantha vivipara (Nutt.) Britt. & Rose *see Escobaria vivipara* (Nutt.) F. Buxb.				
Cotoneaster adpressus Bois.	dwarf cotoneaster	rose	shade to sun	8–12" (20–30 cm)
Cotoneaster apiculatus Rehd. & Wils.	cranberry cotoneaster	rose	shade to sun	24" (60 cm)
Cotoneaster horizontalis var. *perpusillus* Schneid.	dwarf horizontal cotoneaster	rose	east exposure	24–30" (60–75 cm)

U=UPRIGHT ◆ M=MOUNDING ◆ Gr-C=GROUNDCOVER ◆ L=LOOSE ◆ W=WOODY

FORM	BLOOM COLOR	ESTIMATED BLOOM TIME	COMMENTS
M	yellow	all season	Great clumping shade plant for a moist site among ferns and bergenia. Some consider the reseeding habit of this plant "weedy," but seedlings are easy to thin out and the overall effectiveness of this plant is great.
M	blue	throughout summer	Many corydalis cultivars derived from crosses between *C. flexulosa* and other species have blue flowers and may be variously hardy. The Blue Panda is slightly shorter than the common yellow corydalis and is very bright blue with finely divided leaves. Other blue cultivars sold include: ex Corydalis 'China Blue', ex Corydalis 'Balang Mist' and ex Corydalis 'Pere David.'
W, Gr-C	white to pink	early summer	Low ground cover with a creeping habit. Leaves are almost round and turn bright red in fall. Winter berries are red. Special cultivars sold in some areas. Best in areas where snowcover stays longer.
W, M	white to pink	early summer	Small clumping shrub with a juniperlike form. Ideal for the rockery, where its red autumn color and plant form add to the overall effect of the space. Prefers a site with good snowcover in winter.
W, M	white to pink	early summer	Distinctive herringbone-style branching and leaf pattern. Dependable autumn color. Prefers good winter snow.

◆ **Tr**=TRAILING ◆ **M—B**=MOUNDING BUN ◆ **M—U**=MOUNDING UPRIGHT

BOTANICAL NAME	COMMON NAME	FAMILY NAME	IDEAL LOCATION (if particular)	HEIGHT
Cystopteris fragilis (L.) Bernh.	fragile fern	fern	part to full shade	10–14" (25–35 cm)
Delphinium bicolor Nutt.	low larkspur	buttercup	part shade	8–20" (20–50 cm)
Dendranthema weyrichii (Herbich.) Tzvelev.	ground cover mum	daisy	half to full sun; dry	8–10" (20–25 cm)
Dianthus deltoides cvs.	various carnations and pinks	pink	half to full sun	6–8" (15–20 cm)
Dianthus 'Frost Fire'	Frost fire pinks	pink	up to full sun; free-draining soil	4–6" (10–15 cm)
Dianthus gratianopolitanus Vill.	cheddar pink	pink	full sun; open (drought or moist soil)	4–6" (10–15 cm)
Dianthus gratianopolitanus 'Badenia'	Badenia cheddar pink	pink	full sun	4–6" (10–15 cm)

U=UPRIGHT ◆ M=MOUNDING ◆ Gr-C=GROUNDCOVER ◆ L=LOOSE ◆ W=WOODY

FORM	BLOOM COLOR	ESTIMATED BLOOM TIME	COMMENTS
M	n/a	n/a	Delicate fern for shady wedges between rock. Has been observed growing on shear cliff faces in the wild where seepage provides the only moisture, so can probably tolerate drying out between watering or rainfall. Easily moved as a division or even started from spore. Native to North America.
U	blue	early June to mid-July	Excellent prairie and mountain species with brilliant blue flowers on stocky stems. May be difficult to source, as many native plants are, but is worth the effort.
Gr-C	white or pale pink	late summer	Tight ground cover form. 'Pink Bomb' and 'White Bomb' cultivars are available. Both like to creep between rocks.
Gr-C	white to dark pink	from early June	Common ground cover plant for sunny gardens. Often sold as an annual but will survive many winters and rebloom reliably. Flowers are single but numerous with a long bloom period.
M	bright hot pink or carmine	mid-June	Narrow and blue-toned leaves form a low mat. Flowers bloom for about three weeks.
Gr-C	bright double pink	June	Small cushion or mat-forming plant. Flowers are like tiny jewels hovering over narrow blue-toned foliage. Suffers some winter dieback in a fully exposed location.
M	brilliant carmine pink	from May	Tight-mounding or mat-shaped plant with bright flowers throughout the summer.

◆ **Tr**=TRAILING ◆ **M—B**=MOUNDING BUN ◆ **M—U**=MOUNDING UPRIGHT

BOTANICAL NAME	COMMON NAME	FAMILY NAME	IDEAL LOCATION (if particular)	HEIGHT
Dianthus microlepis Boiss.	n/a	pink	full sun	4–6" (10–15 cm)
Dianthus neglectus see *Dianthus pavonius*				
Dianthus pavonius Tausch.	n/a	pink	up to full sun	2–4" (5–10 cm)
Dianthus simulans Stoj. & Stef.	n/a	pink	up to full sun	2–4" (5–10 cm)
Dicentra eximia Torr.	fern leaf bleeding heart	bleeding heart	shade; moist	12" (30 cm)
Dodecatheon conjugans E. Greene	native shooting star	primula	part sun	8" (20 cm)
Dodecatheon pulchellum (Raf.) Merrill.	native shooting star	primula	part sun	8" (20 cm)
Douglasia montana A. Gray.	douglasia	primula	part to full sun	2" (5 cm)
Draba aizoides L.	draba	mustard	part to full sun	2–4" (5–10 cm)

U=UPRIGHT ◆ M=MOUNDING ◆ Gr-C=GROUNDCOVER ◆ L=LOOSE ◆ W=WOODY

FORM	BLOOM COLOR	ESTIMATED BLOOM TIME	COMMENTS
M–B	pink	occasional throughout spring and summer	Very tight-foliage mounding plant with grey-green leaves. Plant form is more significant than the occasional and infrequent flowers.
M	pale pink to purplish red	from June	Very small-mound tufted plant with grey-green leaves. One of the best species for the rock garden.
M–B	pink	throughout spring and summer	Plant forms a tight clump with only occasional blooms in cultivation. Leaves are blue-grey, and flowers sit on the leaves.
M	white or pink	throughout summer	Plant forms a loose mound with continuous bloom. Great for the shady rock garden.
U	pink	May	Tight mat leaves and blooms spring from between rock or other tufted plants. Plant dies back in summer heat, so mark the location or have other plants overgrowing its spot during the summer to avoid a hole.
U	pink	spring	Blooms and habit are very similar to *D. conjugans* E. Greene.
Gr-C	pink	late May to June	Tight ground cover with long-lasting bright pink blooms. A choice alpine plant.
M–U	yellow	late April to mid-May	Flowers are held in clumps above the mounding foliage. Very early and worthwhile addition to the rock garden.

◆ **Tr**=TRAILING ◆ **M—B**=MOUNDING BUN ◆ **M—U**=MOUNDING UPRIGHT

BOTANICAL NAME	COMMON NAME	FAMILY NAME	IDEAL LOCATION (if particular)	HEIGHT
Draba oligosperma Hook	draba	mustard	part to full sun	up to 4" (10 cm)
Draba paysonii Macbr.	draba	mustard	part to full sun	up to 2.5" (6 cm)
Draba rigida Willd.	draba	mustard	part to full sun	up to 2.5" (6 cm)
Dryas octopetala L.	mountain avens	rose	full sun; exposed dry sites	2" (5 cm)
Edraianthus graminifolius (L.) A. D.C.	grassy bells	bluebell	part shade	4" (10 cm)
Epimedium x *rubrum* Morr.	epimedium	barberry	shade; moist soil	up to 10" (25 cm)
Erigeron compositus Pursh.	fleabane	daisy	up to full sun	2–6" (5–15 cm)
Eriogonum umbellatum Torr.	umbrella plant	buckwheat	dry open areas	4–6" (10–15 cm)
Escobaria vivipara (Nutt.) F. Buxb.	cushion or ball cactus	cactus	full sun; crevices	up to 2" (5 cm)

U=UPRIGHT ◆ M=MOUNDING ◆ Gr-C=GROUNDCOVER ◆ L=LOOSE ◆ W=WOODY

FORM	BLOOM COLOR	ESTIMATED BLOOM TIME	COMMENTS
M–U	yellow	late April to May	Flowers are held in clumps above the mounding foliage. Native to the Rocky Mountains. Found in dry alpine slopes and screes. Very early blooming.
M	yellow	late April to May	Tight native perennial found in alpine screes. Very early blooming.
M–B	yellow	late April to May	Tight-mounding perennial from Armenia and Turkey.
Gr-C	pale cream; white seed heads	June or July	Very tight woody ground cover with glossy leaves and oversized flowers. Useful in a wide range of conditions but especially in dry sloping or rock crevice areas as a ground cover. Native to arctic and alpine areas of the northern hemisphere.
Gr-C	blue	June	Tight ground cover with small globelike flowers.
Gr-C	flowers not significant	summer	Grown for its large spearlike leaves with medium texture and dark pink veins. Provides a nice transition between shrubs and smaller rockery plants and is a very good ground cover in a shady site.
M	white	spring to autumn	Plant forms small clump of greyish leaves. Found in alpine and prairie habitats.
M	yellow	summer	Small, almost white-leaved, clump-forming plant found in alpine and prairie habitats. Native from British Columbia to Colorado.
M	bright purplish red	summer	Small globelike cactus covered with spines. Native to stony ground in the prairies.

◆ **Tr**=TRAILING ◆ **M–B**=MOUNDING BUN ◆ **M–U**=MOUNDING UPRIGHT

BOTANICAL NAME	COMMON NAME	FAMILY NAME	IDEAL LOCATION (if particular)	HEIGHT
Eunomia oppositifolium see *Aethionema oppositifolium*				
Euphorbia epithymoides Jacq. *see E. polychroma*				
Euphorbia polychroma Kerner.	cushion spurge	spurge	dappled bright light	12" (30 cm)
Euphorbia myrsinites L.	n/a	spurge	full sun; dry slope	4" (10 cm)
Festuca glauca Vill.	blue fescue cultivars	grass	up to full sun	up to 12" (30 cm)
Festuca ovina var. *glauca* see *Festuca glauca* Vill.				
Galium odoratum (L.) Scop.	sweet woodruff	gardenia	shade; moist	up to 12" (30 cm)
Gentiana acaulis L.	stemless gentian	spring gentian	widely adapted	2.5–3" (6–8 cm)
Gentiana bavarica L.	gentian	gentian	dappled to bright light	2.5–3" (6–8 cm)

U=UPRIGHT ◆ M=MOUNDING ◆ Gr-C=GROUNDCOVER ◆ L=LOOSE ◆ W=WOODY

FORM	BLOOM COLOR	ESTIMATED BLOOM TIME	COMMENTS
M	bright yellow with lemon-lime bracts	mid-May	Plant forms an almost perfect mound. Very striking plant for bright early color. Blooms overlap beautifully with those of the brilliant blue *Gentiana acaulis*.
Gr-C	yellow-green bracts	May	Leaves form rigid, blue-green whorls on stems. Blooms for about three weeks. Allow this plant to reseed because it may be shortlived on the prairies.
M	flowers not significant	n/a	Plant forms radiating clumps of blue leaves. Adds very distinctive form and texture to the rock garden.
Gr-C	white	summer	Ground cover for transition areas between larger shrubs and open, sunny areas in the garden, or for north-facing moist gardens.
Gr-C	brilliant blue	late May to late June	Leaves make a glossy compact mat less than 2" (5 cm) tall with flowers standing erect above the glossy foliage for three weeks. An essential addition to every rock garden on the prairies.
Gr-C	dark blue	May	Leaves are at the base of the flowers on short stems. Blooms last about three weeks.

◆ **Tr**=TRAILING ◆ **M—B**=MOUNDING BUN ◆ **M—U**=MOUNDING UPRIGHT

BOTANICAL NAME	COMMON NAME	FAMILY NAME	IDEAL LOCATION (if particular)	HEIGHT
Gentiana kesselringii Reg	gentian	gentian	dappled to half sun	10–14" (25–35 cm)
Gentiana kochiana Perrier & Song. *see Gentiana acaulis* L.				
Gentiana loderi Hook.	gentian	gentian	part shade; moist organic soil	10–18" (25–45 cm)
Gentiana parryi Engelm.	gentian	gentian	dappled to bright light	8–12" (20–30 cm)
Gentiana septemfida Pall.	fall gentian	gentian	dappled sun; lime-free soil	6–12" (15–30 cm)
Gentiana septemfida Pall. var. *lagodechiana*	gentian	gentian	dappled sun to bright light; lime-free soil	6–12" (15–30 cm)
Gentiana sino-ornata Balf.	gentian	gentian	dappled shade; lime-free soil	prostrate stems to 6" (15 cm)
Gentiana verna L.	spring gentian	gentian	dappled shade to full sun	leaves to 1.2" (3 cm)
Gentiana walujewii var. *see Gentiana kesselringii* Reg.				

FORM	BLOOM COLOR	ESTIMATED BLOOM TIME	COMMENTS
L	white or pale blue	August to September	Lower leaves are .5–.75" (1–1.5 cm) wide and straplike with small flowers on the stem ends.
L	medium to dark blue	July to August	Looks a lot like *G. septemfida* except the stems are wiry and dark brown and somewhat more upright. Flowers at stem ends.
L	medium blue	early to midsummer	Plant tends to flop over and ascend—that is the stems lay flat and then the tips reach upward—rather than maintain a mounded form. Backside of campanula-like blooms are white to green, while inner petal edges are bright blue and fringed between notches.
L	blue	late August to September	Stems have leafy whorls. Leaves are glossy. Flowers are in clusters.
L	blue	September	Stems have leafy whorls and solitary flowers. Leaves are glossy.
L	blue with pale center	September	Rosettes form with large blooms. Many cultivars are available.
Gr-C	blue	late May	Extremely small ground cover form of brilliant blue gentian. Smaller than *G. acaulis*.

◆ **Tr**=TRAILING ◆ **M—B**=MOUNDING BUN ◆ **M—U**=MOUNDING UPRIGHT

BOTANICAL NAME	COMMON NAME	FAMILY NAME	IDEAL LOCATION (if particular)	HEIGHT
Geranium cinereum Cav.var. *cinereum* x 'Ballerina'	ballerina geranium	geranium	up to full sun; well-drained soil	6–8" (15–20 cm)
Geranium dalmaticum Rech.	geranium	geranium	up to full sun; well-drained soil	6–8" (15–20 cm)
Geum coccineum 'Borisii' *see Geum coccineum* 'Werner Arends'				
Geum coccineum Sibth & Sm 'Werner Arends'	geum	rose	up to full sun	up to 12" (30 cm)
Globularia cordifolia L.	globularia	globularia	part shade	1–2" (2–5 cm)
Gypsophila repens L.	creeping baby's breath	pink	full sun; dry site	6–8" (15–20 cm)
Haberlea rhodopensis Friv.	haberlea	African violet	shade and shelter	4–6" (10–15 cm)

U=UPRIGHT ◆ M=MOUNDING ◆ Gr-C=GROUNDCOVER ◆ L=LOOSE ◆ W=WOODY

FORM	BLOOM COLOR	ESTIMATED BLOOM TIME	COMMENTS
M	pink	early June to early September	Long flowering. Color may continue into autumn if the season is long. Many forms of *G. cinereum* are available.
M	pink	July	Excellent prairie rockery plant with fall color from leaves that change to red during cool evenings in September.
M	orange	mid- to late May	Mounding plant with bright orange flowers. Other forms are almost red or yellow. Double and single forms are available—this particular cultivar is a double form. Easy, old-fashioned and reliable.
Gr-C	purple	early summer	Ground-hugging plant with upright globe-like flowers. Gradually creeps to 24–30" (60–75 cm) in diameter.
M	pink or white	late May or June	Mat-forming, silver-leaved, clumping perennial with a slight spraylike effect. Extremely tough. Will readily reseed.
M	pale mauve	late spring	Somewhat tender plant related to African violets. Suited to the shelter of cracks and crevices between rocks where rain will not fall directly on the crown. Leaves are hairy and look similar to Ramonda's. Native to the Balkans.

◆ **Tr**=TRAILING ◆ **M—B**=MOUNDING BUN ◆ **M—U**=MOUNDING UPRIGHT

BOTANICAL NAME	COMMON NAME	FAMILY NAME	IDEAL LOCATION (if particular)	HEIGHT
Hepatica nobilis Mill.	hepatica	buttercup	shade	6–8" (15–20 cm)
Hepatica transsilvanica Fuss.	hepatica	buttercup	shade	6" (15 cm)
Heuchera cylindrica Dougl.	alum root	saxifrage	full sun; exposed; dry;	8–10" (20–25 cm); 10–20" (25–50 cm) in bloom
Heuchera micrantha Douglas ex Lindl. 'Palace Purple'	purple palace coral bells	saxifrage	shade to full sun; moist organic soil	10–18" (25–45 cm)
Heuchera cv. 'Amethyst Myst'	amethyst myst coral bells	saxifrage	shade to half sun; organic soil	10–18" (25–45 cm)

U=UPRIGHT ◆ M=MOUNDING ◆ Gr-C=GROUNDCOVER ◆ L=LOOSE ◆ W=WOODY

FORM	BLOOM COLOR	ESTIMATED BLOOM TIME	COMMENTS
M	white to purple	within a few weeks of snowmelt	Brilliant large clusters of flowers. Like other hepaticas, this one is sometimes semi-evergreen in nature with leaves surviving under a good snowcover. When leaves perish, the large purple (occasionally white) flowers make a dense clump before new leaves form. Flowers are daisy-like with a buttercup cluster of white anthers in the center. Excellent choice for the early spring rock garden.
M	purple to mauve	within a few weeks of snowmelt	Small clumps of flowers appear before the leaves. Ideal for the shady rock garden. Occasionally the leaves are evergreen and overwinter under good snowcover. Flowers have a form similar to *H. nobilis*, *H. americana* and *H. acutiloba*.
M	creamy yellow	June to July	Leaves are broad and mounding. Flowering stalks are tall and thin. Glossy leaves are a highlight, and pale cream petals reflect other soft colors. *H. richardsonii* is a hardy native choice.
M—U	white	June to late summer	Dainty white flowers sit on tall stems above foliage. Dark purple leaves form uniform mounds that contrast well with pastel colors nearby. Other worthy cultivars are Pewter Veil and Snowflake.
M—U	white	June to late summer	Blooms are held on tall stems above foliage that forms a loose clump or mound. Leaves are mottled silver on top and deep reddish pink below. Contrasts nicely with white, soft pink, blue or yellow neighbors.

◆ **Tr**=TRAILING ◆ **M—B**=MOUNDING BUN ◆ **M—U**=MOUNDING UPRIGHT

BOTANICAL NAME	COMMON NAME	FAMILY NAME	IDEAL LOCATION (if particular)	HEIGHT
Hosta spp. and cvs. Tratt.	hosta	lily	shade	6–24" (15–60 cm)
Hylotelephium cauticolum H. Ohba.	sedum cauticola	crassula	sunny; dry	4–6" (10–15 cm)
Hylotelephium ewersii H. Ohba.	sedum ewersii	crassula	up to full sun; tolerates drought	8" (20 cm)
Hymenoxys acaulis see *Tetraneuris acaulis* Greene.				
Iberis sempervirens L. 'Snowflake'	snowflake candytuft	mustard	half sun	12" (30 cm)
Iris cristata Sol. 'Navy Blue'	navy blue iris	iris	half to full sun	6–8" (15–20 cm)
Iris reticulata Bieb. cvs.	*Iris reticulata* hybrids	iris	half to full sun	6" (15 cm)

FORM	BLOOM COLOR	ESTIMATED BLOOM TIME	COMMENTS
M–U	white to mauve	summer	Blooms are held on tall stalks above foliage. Available in extremely dwarf forms as well as very large forms with foliage patterns from striped to solid. Variegated in blue tones through to yellow and white. Offers coarse texture and interest in a woodland or shady rock garden. Avoid large cultivars and choose hostas sold for their small size and interesting foliage.
M	pink	summer	Rosettes of succulent blue leaves offer an attractive texture throughout the year. Fit between rock crevices or let emerge from rock walls.
M	pink	summer	Succulent blue leaves are ideal for a long season of interest. Makes a compact mound with colorful contrast between foliage and flower.
M	white	May to June	Evergreen plant with evenly mounded form and complete cover of white blooms. May need shelter from direct sun in winter especially where snowcover is scant.
U	blue	May	One of the several good irises for upright form in the rock garden.
U	blue to purple	May	Dwarf iris for a hardy spot of color in early spring. Fall planted.

◆ **Tr**=TRAILING ◆ **M—B**=MOUNDING BUN ◆ **M—U**=MOUNDING UPRIGHT

BOTANICAL NAME	COMMON NAME	FAMILY NAME	IDEAL LOCATION (if particular)	HEIGHT
Iris sibirica L.	Siberian iris	iris	up to half sun	12–24" (30–60 cm)
Jovibarba spp.	hen and chicks	crassula	exposed, sunny, dry	2" (5 cm)
Juniperus horizontalis Moench. 'Motherlode'	motherlode horizontal juniper	pine	half to full sun	4–6" (10–15 cm)
Juniperus squamata Buch. -Ham. ex D. Don 'Blue Star'	blue star juniper	pine	half to full sun	16" (40 cm)
Knautia macedonica Griseb.	n/a	teasel	part sun	up to 18" (45 cm)
Lamium maculatum L.	dead nettle, lamium	mint	shade; moist organic soil	4–6" (10–15 cm)

FORM	BLOOM COLOR	ESTIMATED BLOOM TIME	COMMENTS
U	blue	late May to June	Keep to back of garden or order shorter cultivars for midpoint accents in the garden. Texture of Siberian iris is unsurpassed in any garden. Fall or spring planted.
M, Gr-C	yellow	midsummer to July	Rosettes of leaves are monocarpic which means they die after they flower. Very similar to the genus Sempervivum and many people still group the two genera.
W	n/a	n/a	Ground cover juniper from a native North American species. Offers unusual bright yellow foliage and a seasonal color change to orange in the fall. Like the other horizontal species of juniper, it will take on a bronze or purple tone later in fall. Maximum spread is 6.5' (2 m).
W	n/a	n/a	Small mounding juniper with white lines on the underside of needles, which make the plant appear to sparkle. Offers good compact form and habit for a year-round green-blue effect.
U	dark maroon	July to August	Tall perennial for the back of the garden where the flowers add late summer color.
Gr-C	white to pink	late May	Good ground cover for the shady rock garden. Leaf color adds interest in low light areas. All appear hardy, especially the very attractive 'Aureum' with its bright yellow-green leaves. 'White Nancy' has silver leaves with a thin green edge and white blooms but may not be as vigorous in prairie gardens. 'Chequers' has broader leaves with a thin silver stripe.

◆ **Tr**=TRAILING ◆ **M—B**=MOUNDING BUN ◆ **M—U**=MOUNDING UPRIGHT

BOTANICAL NAME	COMMON NAME	FAMILY NAME	IDEAL LOCATION (if particular)	HEIGHT
Larix laricina 'Newport Beauty'	Newport beauty larch	pine	part to full sun	24" (60 cm) in ten years
Leontopodium alpinum Cass.	edelweiss	daisy	up to full sun; tolerates poor soil; dry	8" (20 cm)
Leucanthemum x *superbum* (J. Ingram) Bergmans ex Kent. 'Snow Lady'	snow lady shasta daisy	daisy	from dappled shade to bright sun	12" (30 cm)
Lewisia cotyledon Robinson	lewisia	portulaca	afternoon shade	up to 8" (20 cm)
Lewisia nevadensis Robinson	lewisia	portulaca	some shade; dry	up to 4" (10 cm)
Lewisia rediviva Pursh.	bitterroot	portulaca	dry	up to 2" (5 cm)
Lewisia tweedii Robinson	lewisia	portulaca	part to full sun	up to 2" (5 cm)

U=UPRIGHT ♦ M=MOUNDING ♦ Gr-C=GROUNDCOVER ♦ L=LOOSE ♦ W=WOODY

FORM	BLOOM COLOR	ESTIMATED BLOOM TIME	COMMENTS
W	n/a	n/a	Compact round mound originally from a witch's broom. Like all larches, Newport Beauty is deciduous.
M	white	July	Small nonshowy flowers are surrounded by feltlike decorative leaves so the effect is long-lasting in the garden.
M	white with yellow center	mid- to late June	These compact white daisies are common but hardy. They bloom for three to five weeks.
M–U	pinks	late May to early July	Showy plant that may be shortlived on the prairies because it is evergreen and has fleshy leaves so will not tolerate drying out completely. Needs to be planted at an angle or in a rock crevice where rain cannot fall directly into the center crown. Amazing colors make it worthwhile even as an annual in the rock garden.
M	white to pink	April to May	Very tiny lewisia with relatively large showy flowers. From the Rocky Mountains south to New Mexico.
M	white to pink	April to May	Very tiny plant with leaves that wither as the flowers emerge, which makes the blooms look like they are sitting on soil or mulch. North American alpine plant from higher elevations.
M	pink	May to June	Large fleshy leaves to 3" (8 cm) grow in a clump. Ideally suited to dry crevice gardens. Flowers are extremely showy, but plant may be shortlived, becoming dormant in the summer.

◆ **Tr**=TRAILING ◆ **M—B**=MOUNDING BUN ◆ **M—U**=MOUNDING UPRIGHT

BOTANICAL NAME	COMMON NAME	FAMILY NAME	IDEAL LOCATION (if particular)	HEIGHT
Linum flavum L.	golden flax	flax	part to full sun	12" (30 cm)
Lychnis alpina L.	lychnis	pink	part to full sun	2–6" (5–15 cm)
Lysimachia nummularia L.	creeping Jenny	primula	part sun to almost full shade	1–1.5" (2–4 cm)
Omphalodes verna Moench.	creeping forget-me-not	borage	shade to part sun	4–6" (10–15 cm)
Opuntia fragilis (Nutt.) Haw.	prickly pear cactus	cactus	full sun; excellent drainage	6–8" (15–20 cm)
Opuntia polyacantha Haw.	prickly pear cactus	cactus	full sun; excellent drainage	6–10" (15–25 cm)
Papaver alpinum L.	alpine poppy	poppy	up to full sun	8–10" (20–25 cm)

U=UPRIGHT ◆ M=MOUNDING ◆ Gr-C=GROUNDCOVER ◆ L=LOOSE ◆ W=WOODY

FORM	BLOOM COLOR	ESTIMATED BLOOM TIME	COMMENTS
M	yellow	June to late July	Very bright golden flowers. Somewhat coarser and more mounded than the blue flax seen on the prairies.
U	pink	June to July	Shortlived but brilliant pink perennial that reseeds and thrives in almost any soil and moisture condition.
Gr-C	yellow	July	Tight rock-hugging ground cover for a large crevice or wide flagstone cracks. Will also creep over large rocks or walls. The cultivars 'aurea' and 'goldilocks' contrast dramatically with dark rocks.
Gr-C	blue	May to early June	Vigorous ground cover with clear blue flowers that are distinctive and reliable.
Gr-C	pale yellow	June	Stem segments on this native prairie cactus are nearly circular with 3–5 spines in each clump. Thrives in grasslands and clay flats. Very appropriate in a dry rock garden, especially on a south-facing slope.
M	bright yellow fading to bronze	June	Stem segments on this leafless native prairie cactus are round with spines in clumps of 5–9. Native habitat is prairie grassland and denuded areas, so will thrive in exposed prairie rock gardens.
M	white, yellow, orange	June	Small grey-leaved poppy that may be short-lived but will definitely reseed and appear in various pockets in the garden. It will cross with the larger Icelandic poppies if the two plants are in bee pollination range, so grow only one or the other.

◆ **Tr**=TRAILING ◆ **M—B**=MOUNDING BUN ◆ **M—U**=MOUNDING UPRIGHT

BOTANICAL NAME	COMMON NAME	FAMILY NAME	IDEAL LOCATION (if particular)	HEIGHT
Papaver kluanensis D. Love	alpine poppy	poppy	fast draining; alpine slopes	2.5–4" (6–10 cm)
Paraquilegia anemonoides Ulbr.	paraquilegia	buttercup	filtered or early daylight; good drainage	2.5–3" (6–8 cm)
Penstemon albertinus Greene	penstemon	snapdragon	full sun	8" (20 cm)
Penstemon hirsutus (L.) Willd. 'Pygmaeus'	penstemon	snapdragon	part shady	6" (15 cm)
Penstemon menziesii Hook.	penstemon	snapdragon	full sun to dappled light; dry	4" (10 cm)
Penstemon pinifolius Greene	penstemon	snapdragon	part shade	8–10" (20–25 cm)
Phacelia sericea A. Gray.	silky scorpionweed	waterleaf	open woods to dry scree	4–10" (10–25 cm)
Phlox divaricata L.	blue phlox	phlox	part shade to almost full shade; moist	8–10" (20–25 cm)

U=UPRIGHT ◆ M=MOUNDING ◆ Gr-C=GROUNDCOVER ◆ L=LOOSE ◆ W=WOODY

FORM	BLOOM COLOR	ESTIMATED BLOOM TIME	COMMENTS
M	lemon yellow	June to early July	May be shortlived and may cross with other poppies, so it is best to place this native Alberta plant in a scree bed well away from other poppies. Allow it to reseed.
M	white to pale lilac	June	Beautiful if somewhat difficult-to-find and shortlived perennial that resembles a columbine's foliage and a white buttercup's flower shape. Very delicate.
Gr-C	blue	May to early June	Beautiful native Rocky Mountain plant with icy blue petals on short stems. Rare in cultivation but occasionally available as seed from seed exchanges.
Gr-C	purple	June to August	Pale purple flowers are numerous and last most of the summer.
Gr-C	pink	July and August	Woody creeping ground cover with blooms at the stem ends. A favorite because of its longlived blooms and glossy green leaves.
U	red	June	Very delicately textured plant with long-lasting scarlet blooms. May be shortlived but is worth growing even if it survives only a few years. Attracts hummingbirds.
M	blue	June to July	Distinctive silvery-leaved Alberta native that may be shortlived but does reseed.
U	blue, white	July	Adds an amazing blue color to the shady part of the garden. Blooms on the prairies at the same time as the taller orange trollius and yellow corydalis, which make great companions. May look messy after blooming, so trim spent blooms.

◆ Tr=TRAILING ◆ M–B=MOUNDING BUN ◆ M–U=MOUNDING UPRIGHT

BOTANICAL NAME	COMMON NAME	FAMILY NAME	IDEAL LOCATION (if particular)	HEIGHT
Phlox hoodii Richardson	moss phlox	phlox	dry, exposed	1–1.5" (2–4 cm)
Phlox subulata L.	moss phlox	phlox	part shady; moderately moist	1.5–2.5" (4–6 cm)
Physaria didymocarpa A. Gray	double bladderpod	mustard	up to full sun	2–3" (5–8 cm)
Picea abies (L.) Karst. 'Gregoryana veitschi'	Gregoryana veitschi dwarf Norway spruce	pine	part shade to full sun	10" (25 cm) x 10" (25 cm)
Picea abies (L.) Karst. 'Little Gem'	little gem dwarf Norway spruce	pine	full sun	10" (25 cm) x 10" (25 cm)
Picea abies (L.) Karst. 'Mucronata'	dwarf Norway spruce	pine	full sun	30" (75 cm) x 20" (50 cm)

U=UPRIGHT ◆ M=MOUNDING ◆ Gr-C=GROUNDCOVER ◆ L=LOOSE ◆ W=WOODY

FORM	BLOOM COLOR	ESTIMATED BLOOM TIME	COMMENTS
Gr-C	white	May	Prairie grassland native well suited to the dry rock garden. Very flat. Usually creeps between pockets of grass. Its spring blooms completely cover the plant.
Gr-C	white to pink	May	Shiny-leaved ground cover with very dense and intensely colorful flowers. Its very showy blooms completely hide the foliage. May also be suited to the front of a nearby perennial border, making a striking visual link to the rockery.
M	yellow	late spring to early summer	Prostrate to low-mounding wild Alberta plant with distinctive silvery leaves and large inflated seed pods. Typically seen on high-elevation open slopes and plains, so is suited to our climate.
W	n/a	n/a	Very dwarf form of Norway spruce with irregular tufts of growth on a mounding form. Takes about ten years to reach height and spread indicated. The various kinds of Norway spruce are generally among the hardiest of spruce in our prairie gardens. The following kinds have been selected for their unique form or features.
W	n/a	n/a	Forms a very tight, round, mound. Possibly the smallest form of Norway spruce. Takes about ten years to reach height and spread indicated.
W	n/a	n/a	Small mounding to upright form with very sharp short needles. Takes about ten years to reach height and spread indicated.

◆ **Tr**=TRAILING ◆ **M—B**=MOUNDING BUN ◆ **M—U**=MOUNDING UPRIGHT

BOTANICAL NAME	COMMON NAME	FAMILY NAME	IDEAL LOCATION (if particular)	HEIGHT
Picea abies (L.) Karst. 'Nidiformis'	nest spruce	pine	full sun	3' (1 m) x 5' (1.5 m)
Picea abies (L.) Karst. 'Ohlendorffii'	Ohlendorf spruce	pine	full sun	8–10' (2.5–3 m)
Picea abies (L.) Karst. 'Pumila'	compact Norway spruce	pine	full sun	30" (75 cm)
Picea abies (L.) Karst. 'Repens'	dwarf Norway spruce	pine	full sun	20" (50 cm) x 3' (1 m)
Picea pungens Engelm. 'St. Mary's Broom'	St. Mary's broom blue spruce	pine	full sun	30" (75 cm)
Picea pungens Engelm. 'Glauca globosa'	dwarf globe blue spruce	pine	full sun	5' (1.5 m)
Picea pungens Engelm. 'Glauca procumbens'	ground cover blue spruce	pine	full sun	8" (20 cm)

U=UPRIGHT ◆ M=MOUNDING ◆ **Gr-C**=GROUNDCOVER ◆ **L**=LOOSE ◆ **W**=WOODY

FORM	BLOOM COLOR	ESTIMATED BLOOM TIME	COMMENTS
W	n/a	n/a	Low flat form with a distinctive dip in the center of the maturing plant—this dip gives the plant its common name. New growth is very bright green.
W	n/a	n/a	Tight conical evergreen with a unique pyramidal form for the small garden. Reaches height indicated in fifteen years.
W	n/a	n/a	Small almost flat form with a slightly mounded shape.
W	n/a	n/a	Another fine cushion-shaped Norway spruce.
W	n/a	n/a	Smallest mounding form of blue spruce. Makes a nice informal clump shape with year-round blue needles. Like the many forms of Norway spruce, the Blue Spruce are also hardy. They are not always bright blue but many are. Listings here include only small or very dwarf forms suited to the rock garden. Will tolerate full wind exposure in low or high elevation gardens.
W	n/a	n/a	Moderately small and very hardy globe spruce with very blue leaves. Demonstrates a tendency to revert to an upright tree. Remove the top leader as it forms to keep the plant in a mound shape. Vibrant color is best viewed in a very sunny location.
W	n/a	n/a	Hardy groundcover with low form that tumbles and spreads over rock surfaces. Spread may reach 6–10' (2–3 m), which is large compared to the truly dwarf cultivars.

◆ **Tr**=TRAILING ◆ **M—B**=MOUNDING BUN ◆ **M—U**=MOUNDING UPRIGHT

BOTANICAL NAME	COMMON NAME	FAMILY NAME	IDEAL LOCATION (if particular)	HEIGHT
Picea pungens Engelm. 'Iseli Fastigiate'	columnar blue spruce	pine	full sun	10–16' (3–5 m)
Picea pungens Engelm. 'Nana'	dwarf Colorado spruce	pine	full sun	3' (1 m)
Picea pungens Engelm. 'Thuem'	compact blue spruce	pine	full sun	30" (75 cm)
Pinus mugo Turra. 'Mops'	mops mugo pine	pine	full sun	30" (75 cm)
Pinus strobus 'Sea Urchin'	sea urchin white pine	pine	full sun	17" (45 cm)
Pinus aristata Engelm. 'Sherwood Compact'	Sherwood compact bristlecone pine	pine	full sun	6.5' (2 m)

U=UPRIGHT ◆ M=MOUNDING ◆ Gr-C=GROUNDCOVER ◆ L=LOOSE ◆ W=WOODY

FORM	BLOOM COLOR	ESTIMATED BLOOM TIME	COMMENTS
W	n/a	n/a	Compact and tall blue-needled form. It is grafted or cloned—it does not grow on its own roots. Trees may grow as tall as a two-story building after 25 years. Width should not exceed 3' (1 m). Remove heavy winter snow that may splay the naturally ascending branches.
W	n/a	n/a	Low mound very similar in shape to the 'Glauca globosa' forms except that this plant has green needles instead of blue. Use it for a hardy contrast in winter to the blue color of the dwarf blue spruce.
W	n/a	n/a	Very low blue form with a spreading habit. Doesn't form a leader like the 'Glauca globosa' and will remain much smaller.
W	n/a	n/a	Slowly growing tight dwarf selection of the mugo pine. Some references imply it develops an upright habit, but it is also listed as the smallest of the mugo pines. Should be hardy across the prairies, but will not tolerate salt splash from passing vehicles.
W	n/a	n/a	This ball-shaped tree is the tightest form of white pine. After 10 years mine is only 12' (30 cm) tall and wide. Soft pale green needles.
W	n/a	n/a	Upright dwarf form native to the Rocky Mountains. Needs some summer shade. Cannot tolerate the intensity of a full western exposure. Requires winter shade from the south or west side. Very dark green leaves. Needles grow in groups of five and are covered with dots of natural white resin.

◆ **Tr**=TRAILING ◆ **M—B**=MOUNDING BUN ◆ **M—U**=MOUNDING UPRIGHT

BOTANICAL NAME	COMMON NAME	FAMILY NAME	IDEAL LOCATION (if particular)	HEIGHT
Primula auricula L.	auricula primula	primula	part shade to full sun; tolerates limy soil (high pH)	8" (20 cm)
Primula cortusoides L.	cortusoides primula	primula	shade; organic soil	leaves to 6" (15 cm); 12" (30 cm) in bloom
Primula denticulata Sm.	drumstick primula	primula	shade to full sun; organic soil	leaves to 10" (25 cm); 8" (20 cm) in bloom
Primula hirsuta All.	primula	primula	full sun; dry scree	4–6" (10–15 cm)
Primula juliae Kuzn.	primula	primula	light shade; moist organic soil	4" (10 cm)
Primula marginata Curtis. cvs.	primula marginata hybrids	primula	sun or shade; dry or moist soil	4–8" (10–20 cm)
Primula rosea Royale.	primula	primula	full sun to shade; dry to moist soil	8" (20 cm)

U=UPRIGHT ◆ M=MOUNDING ◆ Gr-C=GROUNDCOVER ◆ L=LOOSE ◆ W=WOODY

FORM	BLOOM COLOR	ESTIMATED BLOOM TIME	COMMENTS
M	yellow to purple	late April	Fleshy or waxy-leaved plants with very early spring color. Reliable, hardy and easy to grow from cuttings taken right after bloom and set out in the garden (see illustration on page 161).
M–U	pink	late May	Broad leaves with tall spikes of flowers emerging above make this a very exciting plant for the shadier rock garden. May reseed.
M	purple	late April to early May	Blooms appear before the leaves, which are large and coarse in texture. May be divided right after bloom if it becomes overgrown after several years.
M	pink	late April to May	Fleshy leaves make this primula well adapted to the dry rock garden. The pink flowers of this dainty and hardy plant appear on thin stems at the height of the foliage.
Gr-C	dark pink	mid May	Spreads by stolons. Leaf stems are red. Flowers usually nestle between the leaves. Grows in an ever increasing clump. Not fleshy or succulent.
Gr-C	pinky-purple	May to early June	Another primula with fleshy leaves that is easily propagated from cuttings. Flowers are beautiful and dramatic in their season, but the leaves remain exciting all summer into fall with their white scalloped edges. Highly recommended.
M	pink	May	Delicate clumps of leaves may open after flowers have opened. Divide after May bloom.

◆ **Tr**=TRAILING ◆ **M—B**=MOUNDING BUN ◆ **M—U**=MOUNDING UPRIGHT

BOTANICAL NAME	COMMON NAME	FAMILY NAME	IDEAL LOCATION (if particular)	HEIGHT
Primula rubra see *Primula hirsuta*				
Primula warshenewskiana B. Fedtsch.	primula	primula	part shade; moist soil	2–3" (5–8 cm)
Prunella grandiflora L. ssp. *grandiflora*	self heal	mint	part shade to full sun; moist soil	12" (30 cm)
Pulmonaria spp. and cvs. L.	lungwort	borage	shade; moist soil	6–18" (15–45 cm)
Pulsatilla patens (L.) Mill.	prairie crocus	buttercup	part shade to full sun; dry soil	4–6" (10–15 cm)
Pulsatilla vulgaris Mill.	pasque flower	buttercup	part shade; dry to moist soil	8–10" (20–25 cm)

U=UPRIGHT ◆ M=MOUNDING ◆ Gr-C=GROUNDCOVER ◆ L=LOOSE ◆ W=WOODY

FORM	BLOOM COLOR	ESTIMATED BLOOM TIME	COMMENTS
Gr-C	pink	May	Very tiny flowers grow in clusters on short stalks. Flowers are pink with a yellow eye and they emerge before or with the leaves. After a few blooming years, the plant needs dividing or it will lose its vigor. Classic crevice or cool Himalayan plant which is very exciting in the prairie garden.
Gr-C	pinky-purple	midsummer until frost	Heavy-looking ground cover plant with almost continuous bloom. Look for the compact subspecies or this plant may reach 24" (60 cm).
M	pink to blue	April to May	Plant with a variety of heights and textures but always in a mound form with variegated leaves. Leaves are usually speckled white or striped silver. Look for the smaller compact cultivars such as P. longifolia 'Bertram Anderson'.
M	purple	April to late May	Well suited to the gravelly dry soils of most rock gardens, but may be shortlived in cultivation. Start from fresh seed or allow to reseed in garden.
M	purple	May to June	This European introduction is very similar to our native plants and people sometimes confuse them. They are often a richer purple and they bloom longer and more prolifically in our gardens. Enjoy the many cultivars and the early spring color.

◆ **Tr**=TRAILING ◆ **M—B**=MOUNDING BUN ◆ **M—U**=MOUNDING UPRIGHT

BOTANICAL NAME	COMMON NAME	FAMILY NAME	IDEAL LOCATION (if particular)	HEIGHT
Ramonda myconii Rehb.	ramonda	African violet	cracks in rock walls with moist seepage	4–6" (10–15 cm)
Salix arctica Pall.	Arctic willow	willow	thin organic soil with frequent moisture	4" (10 cm)
Salix arenaria L.	silverleaf creeping willow	willow	moist organic or mulched gravelly soils	12–18" (30–45 cm)
Salix repens argentea see *S. arenaria*				
Salix vestita Pursh.	rock willow	willow	shade to sun	up to 5' (1.5 m) in sub-alpine
Saxifraga aizoon Jacq. *see Saxifraga paniculata* Mill.				
Saxifraga aizoon 'Minutifolia' *see Saxifraga paniculata* Mill. 'Baldensis'				
Saxifraga aizoon 'Baldensis' *see Saxifraga paniculata* Mill. 'Baldensis'				

U=UPRIGHT ◆ M=MOUNDING ◆ Gr-C=GROUNDCOVER ◆ L=LOOSE ◆ W=WOODY

FORM	BLOOM COLOR	ESTIMATED BLOOM TIME	COMMENTS
M–U	pale mauve	June	Grows out of rock walls, especially near mountain streams. Cannot tolerate moisture falling directly on its crown. Delicate flowers stretch away from the very flat foliage. A delight, if somewhat tender.
W, Gr-C	n/a	n/a	Very tiny creeping willow found in arctic areas around the world as well as in Alberta's alpine regions. Ideal for the tiny rock garden but largely unavailable in trade.
W	n/a	n/a	Silvery small-leaved shrub with delicate form and additional structure in the rock garden. May not be effective in grey gravel mulched garden because leaves are so pale.
W, M	n/a	n/a	Possibly the author's favorite native Alberta willow. Very attractive and interesting, with round glossy leaves. Has only been seen in the wild, never in a garden center, but still worth dreaming about.

◆ **Tr**=TRAILING ◆ **M—B**=MOUNDING BUN ◆ **M—U**=MOUNDING UPRIGHT

BOTANICAL NAME	COMMON NAME	FAMILY NAME	IDEAL LOCATION (if particular)	HEIGHT
Saxifraga x *arendsii* cvs.	mossy saxifrages	saxifrage	dappled shade	leaves to 2" (5 cm); 8" (20 cm) in bloom
Saxifraga bronchialis L.	saxifrage	saxifrage	part to full sun	2" (5 cm)
Saxifraga canaliculata Boiss. & Reut. ex Engl.	n/a	saxifrage	dappled shade to a few hours of full sun	6–8" (15–20 cm)
Saxifraga cotyledon L.	great alpine rockfoil	saxifrage	full sun tolerated, not required	leaves to 8" (20 cm); 20" (50 cm) in bloom
Saxifraga x *eudoxiana* Kellerer & Sunderm	n/a	saxifrage	dappled shade to full sun	1.2–2" (3–5 cm)
Saxifraga federici-augusti ssp. *grisebachii* D.A. Webb	grisebachi saxifrage	saxifrage	part to full shade; lime or scree	foliage to 2.5" (6 cm); 5" (12 cm) in bloom

U=UPRIGHT ◆ M=MOUNDING ◆ Gr-C=GROUNDCOVER ◆ L=LOOSE ◆ W=WOODY

FORM	BLOOM COLOR	ESTIMATED BLOOM TIME	COMMENTS
M	white to pink	late May	Small mounds of green with a beautiful color, hence the name "mossy." Flowers stand well above foliage. Shortlived plants which need replacing every three to five years when the center dies from moisture sitting on the leaves. Includes 'Peter Pan' and 'Rosenzwerg' cultivars.
Gr-C	white	April to July depending on elevation	Native Alberta saxifrage from our high-elevation rocky outcrops. Flowers have white petals with distinct red dots. Very hardy, not assigned to a "group."
M–B	brilliant white	June to early July	Small mounded plant with individual leaves somewhat curled under. Makes an interesting textural addition to the garden. Belongs to the encrusted group.
M–U	white	June	Large flowering clusters completely cover or spill over foliage. Main clump sometimes dies after blooming, but plant should survive from side rosettes of leaves. Belongs to the encrusted group.
M–B	yellow	May to June	Tight mounding plant for cracks and crevices in the garden. This evergreen is extremely beautiful and hardy. Belongs to the Kabschia group.
M–U	pink	June	Foliage is piled in a mound in this Engleria type of saxifrage. Flowers seem to telescope out of foliage mound along a red leafy stem. Ideal for growing in a crevice.

BOTANICAL NAME	COMMON NAME	FAMILY NAME	IDEAL LOCATION (if particular)	HEIGHT
Saxifraga grisebachii see *Saxifraga federici-augusti* ssp. *grisebachii*				
Saxifraga x *haagii* see S. x *eudoxiana*				
Saxifraga longifolia Lapeyr.	Pyrenean saxifrage	saxifrage	full sun, tolerates some shade; dry crevices	8" (20 cm)
Saxifraga oppositifolia L.	purple mountain saxifrage	saxifrage	full shade to full sun	1–1.5" (2–4 cm)
Saxifraga paniculata Mill. 'Baldensis'	minutifolia saxifrage	saxifrage	part shade to almost full sun	8" (20 cm)
Saxifraga paniculata Mill. 'Brevifolia'	lifelong saxifrage	saxifrage	semi-shade to several hours of sun	panicles to 14–18" (35–45 cm); flowers to 4" (10 cm)
Scutellaria alpina L.	n/a	mint	full sun	10–14" (25–35 cm)

U=UPRIGHT ◆ M=MOUNDING ◆ Gr-C=GROUNDCOVER ◆ L=LOOSE ◆ W=WOODY

FORM	BLOOM COLOR	ESTIMATED BLOOM TIME	COMMENTS
M–U	white	June	Blooms in tall panicles after several years. This exciting plant exhibits grey succulent leaves in tight mounds. Very useful and beautifully textured, but dies after blooming. Belongs to the encrusted group.
M–B	pinky-purple	May to July depending on elevation	Gorgeous dwarf alpine originally from the high mountains of Europe, Asia and North America. Many cultivars are available, and they are stunning in bloom. Thrives in grit or even when planted directly in tufa rock.
M-U	white	June	Easily grown evergreen ground cover perennial with showy white flowers. Excellent for cracks between rocks and garden edges or walls. Also listed as a variety of *S. aizoon* by some references and as *S. aizoon* 'Minutifolia' by others.
M-U	white	June to early July	Dramatically blooming plant that offers a tight rosette with an interesting texture year-round. Belongs to the encrusted group.
U	purple	June to July	Late blooming alpine with soft mauve flowers. Plants tend to be lax, but flowers are upright in terminal racemes (clusters). Tolerates wide range of conditions.

◆ **Tr**=TRAILING ◆ **M—B**=MOUNDING BUN ◆ **M—U**=MOUNDING UPRIGHT

BOTANICAL NAME	COMMON NAME	FAMILY NAME	IDEAL LOCATION (if particular)	HEIGHT
Sedum cauticolum see *Hylotelephium cauticolum*				
Sedum ewersii see *Hylotelephium ewersii*				
Sedum kamtschaticum Fisch.	sedum	crassula	part to full sun	6–8" (15–20 cm)
Sedum spurium Bieb.	sedum	crassula	part to full sun	6–8" (15–20 cm)
Sempervivum arachnoideum L.	hens and chicks, cobweb houseleek	crassula	part to full sun; dry soil	1.5–3" (4–8 cm)
Sempervivum tectorum L.	hens and chicks	crassula	part to full sun	1.5–6" (4–15 cm)

FORM	BLOOM COLOR	ESTIMATED BLOOM TIME	COMMENTS
Gr-C	yellow	June	Sturdy hardy succulent for almost every garden. This plant is not fancy, but is definitely worthwhile.
Gr-C, M	pink	June	Very common ground cover with reliable blooms and interestingly variegated leaf forms. The cultivar 'Tricolor' has leaves that are striped with pink and cream, while 'Variegatum' has leaves that are edged in pink and cream. Other cultivars have leaves that are red-edged, entirely bronze, dark maroon or bright green. Hardy enough to thrive in rock walls or spill over small garden troughs or beds.
Gr-C	pink	July	Rosettes of leaves with cobwebby hairs distinguish this species, which is ideal in any rock garden or even in dry rock walls. Small pieces do not need to be rooted before placement in the garden. Flowers are sometimes overscale, so it may be desirable to remove them early.
Gr-C	pink	July	Very similar to the above species except that there aren't any white hairs covering the leaves. Hardy and succulent plants perfect for adding long season color and strong leaf form. Nomenclature can be confusing. Cultivar or trade names can be more reliable for ordering than the Latin names.

◆ **Tr**=TRAILING ◆ **M—B**=MOUNDING BUN ◆ **M—U**=MOUNDING UPRIGHT

BOTANICAL NAME	COMMON NAME	FAMILY NAME	IDEAL LOCATION (if particular)	HEIGHT
Silene acaulis Jacq.	moss campion	pink	full sun and wind; gravelly alpine soil	5–1" (1–2 cm)
Silene armeria L.	none-so-pretty	pink	part shade to full sun	6–10" (15–25 cm)
Silene schafta S. Gmel. ex Hohento	silene	pink	dappled shade to full sun	leaves to 3–8" (8–20 cm); flowers to 12" (30 cm)
Soldanella alpina L.	soldanella	primula	shade; moist organic soil with drainage	4"(10 cm)
Sisyrinchium montanum E. Greene.	blue-eyed grass	iris	full sun; moist soil	4" (10 cm)
Stachys byzantina K. Koch.	lamb's ears	mint	part to full sun; dry, spilling over rocks	12"(30 cm)

U=UPRIGHT ◆ M=MOUNDING ◆ **Gr-C**=GROUNDCOVER ◆ **L**=LOOSE ◆ **W**=WOODY

FORM	BLOOM COLOR	ESTIMATED BLOOM TIME	COMMENTS
Gr-C	pale to bright pink	May to July depending on elevation	Flat ground cover with narrow glossy leaves. Flowers sit on or just above the leaf surface and bloom sporadically in most seasons.
U	bright pink	late July to frost	Annual for the alpine garden which reseeds readily and blooms vigorously in cracks and crannies.
U	bright pink	July to August	Clump forming, somewhat lax, finely textured perennial with late bloom.
Gr-C	purple	June	May be difficult to grow because of its borderline hardiness and specific soil needs. Try it in sheltered spots. Its flowers, like those of *S. montana*, are fringed and drooping.
U	blue	May to June	Prairie native plant which is difficult to find in garden centers (look for cultivars of the American species) but may appear in your garden as it has in mine. Once in the garden it will reseed and may be divided. Excellent early blossoms. Plants are very adaptable, so move them where you want them.
Gr-C	flowers not significant	n/a	Remove flowers to keep the form and look of this plant uniform in the garden. Attractive and very soft leaves are its best feature. The flowers just make the overall plant look leggy and messy. Tolerates full sun and dry soil but is quite wide in its acceptance of various conditions.

◆ **Tr**=TRAILING ◆ **M—B**=MOUNDING BUN ◆ **M—U**=MOUNDING UPRIGHT

BOTANICAL NAME	COMMON NAME	FAMILY NAME	IDEAL LOCATION (if particular)	HEIGHT
Tetraneuris acaulis Greene.	butte marigold	daisy	sunny; dry slopes	4–8" (10–20 cm)
Thymus praecox Opiz.	mauve or red creeping thyme	mint	part shade to sunny; moist soil	2–4" (5–10 cm)
Thymus serpyllum L.	mother of thyme	mint	part shade to sunny; moist	4–6" (10–15 cm)
Townsendia parryi D.C. Eaton	townsendia	daisy	sunny	2" (5 cm)
Tulipa tarda Stapf.	species tulip	lily	part to full sun	10" (25 cm)

FORM	BLOOM COLOR	ESTIMATED BLOOM TIME	COMMENTS
M	yellow	June	Bright yellow (dandelion-like) mountain daisy on a small mound of foliage. Keep soil low in nutrients as described generally for rock gardens or this plant may grow taller than desired. Some references use *Hymenoxys acaulis* as Latin name.
Gr-C	purple	June	Forms a very tight mat, but it will also creep nicely between rocks along stairs and paths in the rock garden. If it dries out too much it will die in patches.
Gr-C	purple	late May	Somewhat taller ground cover than the *Thymus praecox*. Works well in the gathered moisture at the base of a garden wall.
Gr-C	purple	sporadic until frost	Oversized flowers on this mat of green foliage make the townsendias, especially this prairie native, extremely interesting in the rock garden. Gardeners are forewarned that these plants are very shortlived and seed heads need to be left on the plant so plants will reseed and germinate in the garden for future seasons of blooming. Learning to recognize seedlings is necessary so that they are not weeded out.
U	yellow	May	Vigorous small tulip with upfacing brilliant yellow petals and strap-shaped leaves. Has a habit of reseeding in the garden in available cracks and crannies. These plants go completely dormant in midsummer but should not be dug or disturbed once planted unless they fail to bloom, which would indicate that they need to be lifted and separated.

◆ Tr=TRAILING ◆ M—B=MOUNDING BUN ◆ M—U=MOUNDING UPRIGHT

BOTANICAL NAME	COMMON NAME	FAMILY NAME	IDEAL LOCATION (if particular)	HEIGHT
Veronica armena Boiss. & Huet.	dwarf speedwell	snapdragon	to half shade, prefers light	6" (15 cm)
Veronica prostrata L.	dwarf or creeping speedwell, veronica	snapdragon shade	tolerates half	3" (8 cm)
Veronica repens Clarion ex D.C.	dwarf veronica	snapdragon	full sun to half shade	2–4" (5–10 cm)
Vitaliana primuliflora Bertol.	n/a	primula	to full sun	2" (5 cm)

Plants Not Recommended for the Prairie Rock Garden

Plants with weedy or invasive habits not recommended for the garden include:

Creeping bellflower
Campanula rapunculoides
Invasive roots creep into and around everything. Impossible to eradicate (even with chemicals) once it is established.

Hawkweed
Hieracium spp.
Hawkweed produces an abundance of seeds and has been known to grow in a variety of light and soil conditions, so it is probably too invasive for the rock garden, even though it does have pretty flowers.

Petrorhagia saxifraga
This is messy-looking plant initially reminiscent of babies' breath but later becoming spindly. It reseeds everywhere. Not a valuable addition to texture or color in the garden.

Stone Crop
Sedum acre
Stone crop is so overly vigorous that it becomes entrenched in even the smallest crack between rocks. Even a small fragment of the plant

FORM	BLOOM COLOR	ESTIMATED BLOOM TIME	COMMENTS
Gr-C	blue	June	Compact ground cover which displays finely divided grey leaves. Flowers on short stalks.
Gr-C	blue or pink	May to June	Fairly compact and effective ground cover with full showy blooms on short stalks and simple narrow leaves. This is the author's favorite dwarf veronica.
Gr-C	blue	may to June	Very pale blue flowers and small round leaves. Compact and close to the ground.
M—B	yellow	May	Tight dark green cushion completely hidden by golden flowers in midspring. Extremely showy in bloom and very compact and neat in the garden after the flowering is complete.

can establish itself within a few weeks, making it impossible to eradicate once in place.

Oxe-eye daisy
Leucanthemum vulgare
Considered a noxious weed, this small white daisy is often confused with shasta daisy (Leucanthemum x superbum) which is taller and less invasive than the weed.

Questionable plants include:

Fairies' Thimbles
Campanula cochleariifolia
Widely used because it creeps nicely between rock cracks in walls and provides a great blast of color in late spring or early summer and is fairly easily pulled out, but some gardeners feel it is too invasive for the rock garden.

Corydalis lutea
Reseeds readily and so is reliably hardy and sure to survive in the low light spaces it thrives in. Has been observed in the best prairie gardens so should be considered valuable wherever low light makes rock gardening questionable. Some gardeners dislike its habit of reseeding, but this feature will keep it alive during harsh prairie winters.

Prairie rock
gardeners can
choose from a
wide range of
rock forms and
colors to create
unique and
stunning scenes.

CHAPTER 3

Selecting Rock for the Rock Garden

R OCK GARDENERS CAN EITHER collect or purchase rock for their gardens. I know a man who has built not one but two rock gardens with found rock that he loaded into the trunk of his old Pontiac and brought home over time. This approach, while inexpensive, takes an enormous amount of time and many scouting and collecting trips.

For my garden I paid someone to deliver rock. This may have taken the adventure out of the process, but the costs were up-front—not slowly revealed as shocks needed replacing or hours of time were added up.

Gardening centers and bulk landscape suppliers often stock a wide variety of rock suitable for almost any garden style. Natural tufa, flagstone, fieldstone and river rock are all widely available from the moun-

133

A tiny saxifrage (Saxifraga spp.) less than 2" (5 cm) across grows directly out of a hole drilled in tufa rock.

tains or prairies. However, before choosing the rock to construct your garden, consider the wise advice offered by H. Lincoln Foster in *Rock Gardening:* "A collection of various types of stones, especially those of bright color or freakish shape, may be geologically amusing, but such rocks are always distracting in a rock garden." The key to choosing rock is to ensure that it is appropriate to the style of garden and that the same type of rock is used consistently throughout to strengthen the garden's sense of unity. Remember rock is a framework to which you will add your plant picture.

Tufa

Our own lightweight tufa is a great alternative to imported and unnatural-looking lava, feather and pumice rock. Tufa is a porous rock formed as a deposit from springs or streams. Geologists expand the description by explaining that water must pass through limestone rock and carry dissolved calcium carbonate to the surface, where it will lay down deposits that eventually result in tufa.

For years it was with a sigh and bit of remorse that garden writers would sadly discuss the beauty of tufa rock in the British garden. It was thought to be unavailable in North America and only worth dreaming about. It is now known to be available right here on the prairies wherever moisture comes to the surface. The experience of Des Allen, the geologist consulted for this book, indicates that tufa is probably evident in many more sites than we ever believed possible.

The benefit of tufa is its light weight and porous nature. Available in large chunky pieces or thin slab-like plates, it is easy to move into place in the garden, and it also is soft and easily carved or chipped to create planting pockets. Moisture easily passes through tufa rocks, keeping them moist but not soggy wet, an ideal condition for many plant roots, including lime-tolerant saxifrages, which will germinate

Truckloads of rundle rock were delivered to the Paulson's to build the small rock wall that contributes form and a strong sense of line to their large alpine garden.
(PHOTO BY CLIFF PAULSON)

and grow directly into the tufa when seeds are sprinkled on its surface. Once exposed to the elements, pieces of tufa harden and become quite permanent. In a shade rock garden, tufa will, over time, host beautiful dark green mosses, which soften the bright gold or buff color of recently quarried rock.

The disadvantage to using tufa is that, like sandstone, it can leech lime into the soil, necessitating the careful selection of plants that will tolerate a high pH level. Alternately, the rock garden may require the occasional addition of aluminum sulphate fertilizer to raise acidity.

Limestone

Rocky Mountain peaks are all limestone, so it's not unusual that large quantities should be found in prairie rock gardens. One type of Rocky Mountain limestone quarried for garden use is called Rundle rock.

It is a brown to black shaley limestone material that breaks into easily handled slabs, commonly called flagstone, and that lends itself well to the style of many rock gardens. Rundle rock is mined at Thunderstone quarries near Canmore, Alberta, and is generally readily available through bulk landscape suppliers across the prairies. While it is easy to use and more readily approximates the natural scene, its dark color may pose an aesthetic problem if the garden site is north-facing or in the shade of heavy overhanging trees. In a north-facing garden it may be better to use a lighter colored flagstone, which most commonly means sandstone.

Sandstone

"Farm fieldstone is often so rounded it's hard to make it look natural. You have to look for sedimentary rock such as sandstone,

Unfortunately some of the Paskapoo sandstones do not hold up well over time and begin to crumble in the garden. The small creeping form of bluebell (Campanula betulifolia) *illustrates the value of trailing plants in the rock garden.*

which is laid down in layers, to make a nice outcropping in the garden," commented geologist Desmond Allen when I interviewed him about prairie geology for this book. Sandstone, like Rundle rock, was laid down in layers and is available in flat flaggy pieces that are not only easy to work with but are ideal for constructing natural-looking rock outcrops.

A disadvantage of using sandstone in the garden is that it occasionally disintegrates, a phenomenon sometimes seen in older buildings. Although there are theories explaining this occurrence, there doesn't seem to be a way to predict sandstone's demise. Within a building perhaps only a few rocks will disintegrate. Within a garden, much the same holds true.

A disadvantage of the sandstones available in the Calgary, Alberta, area (known as Paskapoo sandstones) is that they often contain calcium carbonate, a crystalline form of lime. Free lime is injurious to many rock garden plants, which will show their displeasure by becoming pale just between the leaf veins. A quick acid test, which involves pouring a few drops of vinegar on the rock, will tell you if your sandstone contains free lime. If the surface of the rock sizzles in reaction to the acid, free lime is present. If for reasons of availability, economy or aesthetics, you must use sandstone high in free lime, you should experiment to find plants that will tolerate a high pH level. You may find it necessary to monitor plants and add aluminum sulphate fertilizer as needed, especially if your garden design includes acid-loving evergreens and bog plants.

Non-Paskapoo prairie sandstones contain silica grains between the sand granules, which makes them acidic, not basic. These will not react to the acid test and will not unfavorably alter the pH level of the soil around them.

Prairie rock gardeners are encouraged to look for local sandstone bedrock on exposed sites such as river cutbanks or eroded hills. After asking permission from the landowner, you can easily cart sandstone home in manageable slabs that are thankfully not as heavy as denser rocks such as granite.

Fieldstone

Glaciers scraping their way across the prairies tens of thousands of years ago brought rock from the Canadian Shield in the east together with rock from the mountains in the west. Only the hardest rock survived the grinding and dragging of the moving ice. Today, these rocks are commonly called fieldstones by nongeologists, and they are distinguished by their small spherical shape.

Large rocks, known as erratics, may be as large as the house-sized boulders dropped near Okotoks, Alberta. To the east of Calgary, Alberta, fieldstones dropped by the movement of glaciers include crystalline rocks such as granite, gneiss and misaschist. West of Calgary, Rocky Mountain quartzite was dragged east by glaciation. This meets rock from Manitoba in a track running north–south through a point just east of Calgary.

Rocks dropped by glaciers have the advantage of being generally readily available just for the asking from prairie farmers like my father, who are always happy to be rid of them. Various interesting tones are available in a pleasing array of pinks, greys and grey-greens, and it is not unusual for them to host colorful lichens that add incidental color and interest to the garden scene.

A disadvantage of using fieldstones, however, is that the combination of plants and spherical rocks is rarely found in nature. The problem of credibility extends to the use of even a single oversized boulder too often found in gardens. Even though this idea is based on the natural phenomenon of the erratic, large boulders seemingly dropped in a garden without context look as illogical there as they do on the flat prairie. They simply seem too large to have been carried there by any force. If you decide to use fieldstone as your construction material, it may be better to abandon realism and simply focus on creating pleasing groupings of mounded plants that complement the smooth stones.

Another disadvantage of using fieldstones is that putting them back together in a believable geologic formation is a bit like putting Humpty Dumpty back together again. The rocks are not what they were when they were dragged from the mountains or the Shield. This disadvantage of fieldstone may be partially overcome if rocks of similar color and origin are arranged so that the striations within the rock are kept within a uniform plane across the garden.

River Rock

Any stone found in stream beds or along riverbanks may be called river rock. It is geologically varied in origin, but its general shape is the same. River rock has very soft edges (even moreso than fieldstone), resulting from years of erosion by water. River rock is variable in size and has been used often by gardeners for decorative rubblestone walls, paths or fence posts. It does, however, present the same aesthetic problems as fieldstone, so it is not very useful in the rock garden unless it is incorporated into a dry stream bed theme, where it will look geographically correct.

Determining the Amount and Cost of Rock Material

Like any gardening project, a rock garden can cost anywhere from under $1,000 to over $100,000, depending on its size, style and plant materials. For example, my little 100 sq ft (9 sq m) garden built from tufa cost well under $1,000 for mulch, soil, plants and two tons of rock. By contrast, a recently completed large rock feature surrounding a 9000 square foot bungalow cost in excess of $100,000 just for the rock and its placement. The plants, soil, irrigation and labor cost an additional $200,000.

The amount of rock required for your garden will vary according to its surface area and elevation. As a general rule, plan to have approximately 30 percent of the garden's surface area in rock. Thus a 100 sq ft (9 sq m) garden will require at least 30 sq ft (3 sq m) of surface area devoted to rock. The problem, however, is that you can't go to your local garden supply center and purchase 30 sq ft of a product that is typically sold by the pound and ton. Though only the roughest estimate can be made, consider that every 10 sq ft (1 sq m) of garden with an elevation of 3' (1 m) or less will require about 2 tons of heavier rocks of various sizes such as limestone or 800 lbs (363 kg) of much lighter rock such as tufa.

Building a rock wall or stepping stone path requires a different kind of calculation based on uniform spacing between rocks. A wall 12" (30 cm) wide by 24" (60 cm) high by 16' (5 m) long will require approximately 1.5–2 tons of 1" (2.5-cm) thick slab rock. Bear in mind that thicker rock slabs are less expensive than thinner. Slab sandstone or limestone is priced by thickness and weight, with 3–6" (7.5–15-cm) rock costing 50–60 percent less than the equivalent weight of 1" (2.5-cm) -thick slabs. Many gardeners will mix and match these various slab thicknesses to create an interesting wall.

For a stepping stone path, it is advisable to use either 1" (2.5-cm) -thick or 2" (5-cm) -thick slab rock. One ton of 1" (2.5-cm) -rock spaced with 1" gaps between rock will cover approximately 150 sq ft (14 sq m) of surface area while one ton of 2" (5-cm) -rock will cover only half that amount.

Obviously, the cost of rock can vary considerably depending upon the kind of rock. There is no way to know the exact cost of rock available to the home gardener. Unlike shopping for a specific gadget via eBay, shopping for rock is a function of local supply and suppliers, natural availability and the location of the garden in relation to the sources of rock. If a decision is made to purchase rock rather than collect it, check with local landscapers and bulk landscape materials suppliers first.

When planning your purchase of rocks, bear in mind that their weight can be deceptive for their size. An average granite boulder 12 x 12 x 12" (30 x 30 x 30 cm) can weigh up to 125 lb (57 kg) and can be set in place by hand with some help. But a rock 24 x 24 x 24" (60 x 60 x 60 cm) could weigh up to 1,000 lb (454 kg) and can only be set in place by Bobcat or crane. Much lighter tufa rock weighs 15–20 percent the weight of a heavy limestone such as Rundle rock.

If you'll need a crane to place rock, expect to pay $45–$75 per hour. A heavy duty crane may reach distances of 70' (21 m) within your backyard, so it isn't necessary to build the garden right where the rock is dropped, but if your plan calls for smaller rock that will be placed by hand you will want the rock delivered as close to the garden site as possible.

CHAPTER 4

Constructing the Rock Garden

HERE IS A CERTAIN FEAR AND loathing of things unknown. If you have never worked with rock before—or, if like my father, you have only worked to rid your land of rock—considerations both aesthetic and practical may prevent you from enjoying the beauty of rock in your landscape. You might fear creating something that looks more like an unsightly rock pile than a garden, or you might imagine the labor involved to be enormous, or you might believe the price of rock gardens to be prohibitive. Such fears are, however, easily dispelled.

First, putting the chosen rock together in a garden setting with plants and paths should be no more intimidating than constructing any other kind of garden. The only common mistake—evenly placing rock in tombstone fashion in upright rows—can be easily avoided by

Peter Holme's landscape crew builds the Paulson garden from Rundle Rock and specially prepared soil.

141

LEFT:
Llyn Strelau
works on his
Rundle-based
rock garden in
Calgary.

RIGHT: Rodney
Shaver works
with Llyn Strelau
to create a
south-facing rock
outcrop for
various alpines
and rock garden
plants.

After some initial
installation
work, a natural-
looking rock
outcrop begins to
take shape.

sloping the rock into the bed or stacking it into small walls or natural-looking layers. If you studied natural rock outcrops, took photographs and made rough sketches while gathering inspiration during the design phase of developing your rock garden, you are well on your way toward constructing a natural-looking scene.

Secondly, if the rock is enormously heavy, it can easily be moved by a Bobcat or crane rather than a sturdy back. Major boulders can be shifted into place in minutes and with relatively little expenditure. Once these backbone rocks are placed, you can move smaller rock and soil into place by hand. The ultimate result is a garden that will never need replacing, that will suffer little winterkill and will require little maintenance.

Thirdly, if if you find the price of rock prohibitive, use a different rock. Tufa, for instance, is one of the least expensive rocks to choose from when cost and volume are factored in, and fieldstone is free. If using a different kind of rock won't reduce the expense, then consider using the rock differently. Having a short slab rock wall built approximately 24" (60 cm) high and 13' (4 m) long may cost in the order of $1,000.

But the same area could be landscaped in gentle rock and soil layers for less than half the cost of a solid wall.

Preparing the Planting Bed

The first step is to mark out the rock garden area, according to your plan, with a garden hose or length of rope. Rockery plants require excellent drainage, so it is necessary to ensure that the planting bed have an elevation of at least 8" (20 cm) above grade at its lowest point.

The decision to remove existing sod from the planting site will depend upon the elevation and size of the site. If the gardening space is on a slope that provides good drainage it may be necessary to excavate the sod and at least 1" (2.5 cm) of soil so rocks can be positioned into the slope to hold runoff. If the site is large, hand digging may prove too laborious, and it may be wise to rent a sod stripper.

Once the sod is removed check the depth of the remaining topsoil with a spade. If you have at least 1" (2.5 cm) of topsoil remaining, the other constituents of generic soil mix can be spread evenly over the topsoil and mixed with the loam with a rototiller. You may find hand digging therapeutic but it is not as effective as rototilling for mixing the soil components.

If the site is relatively flat it isn't necessary to remove sod before construction. Instead it may simply be sprayed with a grass-killing herbicide. Your local garden center or hardware store can recommend an appropriate formulation. Mark the site carefully, follow the manufacturer's safety precautions and spray only during calm conditions so the herbicide isn't carried outside the planting bed. Start spraying on one edge of the site and work progressively backward to the other so that you are not walking over the sprayed area. Within a few days of spraying, construction can commence.

If you decide not to remove the sod, you'll have to ensure that there is enough rock garden soil over it to avoid accidentally digging up sods when the finished garden is worked in. A depth of over 12" (30 cm) of soil placed over any sod left in place is a minimum amount.

In rare cases, where the topsoil or loam on site is too deep or where it would leave the finished garden too far above grade after the additional soil amendments are added during soil preparation, excess topsoil may be removed after the sod is skimmed or killed off.

Once the site is prepared, you can begin to add rock garden soil and rough grade the site. Rough grading is the general process of moving the soil around to get the general landforms desired. In new landscapes the rough grading may be partially completed before the soil mix is added, but in older land-

Leaf Mold

Bark Fines

Sedge Peat

Shredded Sphagnum Peat

Various low-nutrient sources of organic matter help to amend specially prepared rock garden soil. All these forms of organic matter will also slowly acidify and improve the soil pH. (PHOTO BY GEORGE WEBBER)

scapes the soil is far too compact to move easily unless, of course, your rock garden project is so large that a Bobcat is needed to prepare the site. In these cases, rough grading may be accomplished with the Bobcat before the soil is amended.

Rock Garden Soil

Mixing the soil for a specialty garden space is rather like mixing a cake or making bread. It's right when it feels right. Knowing when it's right requires that you bear in mind the original habitat of the plants that will be featured in your rock garden. Many of these plants are found growing in soil that is often sandy, usually very gravelly and often completely without a typ-

ical soil—clay content. This little detail will help you judge if the soils you are blending are suited to the plants you are growing, so when you're exploring the alpine environment for rock garden inspiration, it's also a good idea to examine the soil conditions supporting the plants.

Experienced and professional rock gardener Panayoti Kelaidis, the Curator of the Alpine Garden within the Denver Botanical Garden, once tried to convince me to completely avoid natural soils in the rock garden. He argued that loam was too rich and would yield plants too lush for the rock garden. Steve Doonan, a visiting guest speaker to the Calgary Rock and Alpine Garden

Sil 9
(Turkey Grit)

1/2" Natural
(Washed)

10 mm Rundle Sand
(Unwashed)

Gyra Sand Chips
(Washed)

Society, also avoids natural soil wherever possible because the heavy coastal rains in his Seattle garden would leave his clay-based soil too sodden.

Both are right for their regions, but, once again, what holds for the rest of the continent doesn't hold for the prairies, where rock gardens generally require some loam in the soil mixture. Prairie rock garden soil should contain limited loam combined with other materials such as gravel, sharp sand or nutrient-poor organic matter such as bulk peat moss (not shredded bagged sphagnum) or screened composted bark mulch (not rich garden compost or composted manure). While garden composts are high in organic material, they also can be fairly high in nutrients and trigger lush tall growth in rockery plants. Lincoln Foster, in his classic book *Rock Gardening* agrees, suggesting that gardeners should add only low fertility organics such as leaf mold because "the usual compost pile is too rich and may contain an abundance of weed seeds."

Generic Soil Mixes for Rock Gardens

A basic prairie rock garden soil mix will contain the following:

1 part loam

1 part washed gravel

1 part coarse sand (5 mm)

1 part composted peat or fine bark chips

Inorganics such as the various types of grit and gravel are essential soil amendments in the rock garden but also make excellent surface mulches to modify soil temperature and moisture regimes.
(PHOTO BY GEORGE WEBBER)

The loam component of the rock garden soil mix should contain approximately 40 percent sand, 20 percent clay and 40 percent silt. You should recognize that what is sold as loam by garden suppliers often differs considerably from this ideal ratio. If a proper loam is unavailable, you may be wise to limit the natural soil component of the rock garden to less than 20 percent of the total mix. If in doubt use the squeeze test as an indicator of the composition of your rock garden soil mix. A small moist clump of soil should not hold together when rolled between your fingers. If it does, the clay content in the soil is too high.

The gravel and coarse sand components of rock garden soil are often referred to as the grit component. Grit helps supply fast drainage and large numbers of air spaces between the soil particles. Some gardeners prefer fine round gravel to sharp gravel, which, due to its flat edges, may compact as the soil settles. Any gravel added should definitely be washed and screened to avoid accidentally adding the fine clay and silt particles found in unwashed gravels.

The organic component of rock garden soil is provided by low-nutrient forms of organic matter. The most commonly seen sources are ground or composted bark or bulk shredded peat. These organic materials contribute to water-holding capacity but also balance soil pH by adding their acidic chemistry to the mix.

If attempting to replicate a woodland or shady mountain scene complete with stream, your soil mix will be overlaid with decomposed leaf mold and sphagnum moss, but its basic composition remains more or less the same as that required for a sunny site. Excellent drainage is as important in the shade rock garden as it is in sun and the mixes suggested here will work for either condition.

If an individual plant has a specific need for acidic soil or more moisture, the little pocket of soil where that plant is installed may be modified individually. Bog peat is usually both acidic and water holding, so it is used if the plant requires these conditions. For the creation of a bog area within a rock garden it may be necessary to line the area with clay, plastic or rubber to slow down the water drainage. This, however, can be a complicated process and is not recommended for the beginning gardener.

Rock Garden Soil Options

These soil mixes have been devised by veteran rock gardeners associated with the Calgary Rock and Alpine Garden Society for special conditions or as personal favorites. They contain variations upon the generic rock garden soil mix and may prove very useful if the ingredients are readily available in your area.

FRANK DORSEY'S BEST ALPINE POT MIX

1 part loam

1 part peat or compost

1 part grit (mixed sizes)

For some saxifrages Frank prefers a mix with 80 percent grit and 20 percent loam.

ZOLTAN GULYAS' STANDARD ALPINE MIX

1 part loam

1 part 5 mm washed sharp sand

1 part 7 mm crushed slate

1 part peat

Zoltan is a very precise gardener and a grower of interesting alpine and rock garden plants.

WILHELM ROTH'S STANDARD ALPINE SOIL

1 part 7 mm washed gyra rock (Gyra is also sometimes called rock chips and is fine washed sharp-edged pea gravel that has flat edges resulting from its being crushed before being screened).

1 part loam

1 part 5 mm washed sand

1 part uncompressed peat moss available from bulk suppliers of landscape material (differs slightly from compressed, shredded peat available in bags).

Wilhelm's mix is ideal for scree—styled gardens. The only time he amends this mix is for his stemless gentian *(Gentian acaulis)* bed, where he prefers more peat moss and richer loam.

RODNEY SHAVER'S STANDARD SOIL MIX

1 part poor loam (very sandy is preferred)

1 part 3 mm crushed Rundle stone

All Rod's beds are topdressed with sifted Rundle rock (a fine shaley slate available from the Rocky Mountains).

BOB STADNYK'S FAVORITE ALPINE SOIL

2 parts sand (5 mm)

1 part loam

1 part bark or peat

SHEILA PAULSON'S ALPINE GARDEN SOIL

1 part peat

1 part loam

2 parts #9 red/brown granite pebbles (also called sil 9 or turkey grit)

Sheila's mix no doubt contributed to her rock garden being selected one of the Calgary Horticulture Society's gardens of distinction.

Determining Rock Garden Soil Quantities

It is one thing to determine the soil mix you need for your home rock garden and quite another thing to figure out how much of the stuff you actually need to order. Don't make a wild guess about the volume of soil mix required. Calculating the accurate figure is not all that difficult. Calculations are made using the imperial system because this is still the way soil is commonly sold.

1. Calculate the total surface area of the rock garden by multiplying width times length.

2. Determine the depth of soil mix required.

3. Multiply the total surface area by the soil mix depth in square feet to calculate the total number of cubic feet of soil mix required.

4. Divide the total number of cubic feet by 27 (the number of cubic feet in a cubic yard) to determine the number cubic yards of soil mix required.

EXAMPLE:

18' (width) x 25' (length) = 450 square feet (total surface area)

450 (total surface area) x .67' (planting soil depth) = 300 cubic feet

300 cubic feet ÷ 27 = 11 cubic yards of soil mix

The chart below provides a quick reference for determining the number of cubic yards of soil mix required.

Truck size for home deliveries is either up to 10 yards or up to 15 yards. Don't order quantities just above the maximum load size because trucking is priced per delivery. It would be silly to order 16 yards, for instance, because that would require one full truck plus an extra truck carrying only a yard of soil.

Soil Preparation

Large quantities of soil may be ordered premixed from reliable suppliers of bulk landscape product, but you may prefer to mix your own soil, especially if certain elements of the final mix are not available from your supplier. If the amount of soil needed is more than can be mixed in a wheelbarrow, it is best to employ the large-batch mixing method. A large rip-proof tarp is laid on the ground near the delivered piles of materials, and the desired quantity of each constituent in the mix is added to one end of the tarp. The tarp is then pulled over on itself several times to mix the ingredients uniformly.

Quick Reference Chart for Various Soil Depths

Square feet of garden surface area	Depth of soil or mulch	Divide total square feet by	Number of cubic yards of soil needed (rounded to nearest yard)
500	2"	162	3
500	4"	81	6
500	6"	54	9
500	8"	40.5	12
500	10"	32.4	15
500	12"	27	19

Before constructing their alpine rock garden, Sheila and Cliff Paulson had a vegetable garden in their east and south-facing backyard. (PHOTO BY SHEILA AND CLIFF PAULSON)

Setting the Rock

Keeping the amount of visible rock to about 30 percent of the garden space is about right. Any more than that and the area will be seen as rocks with a few plants rather than as a rock garden. Any less and the rock impact will be too minimal to really make a contribution.

The goal when setting rock is to keep the overall look natural within the style of rock garden desired. If, for example, large flat slabs of sandstone are used to create a coulee rock outcrop, they will look most realistic if they are sloping back into the mound. This angle will allow the moisture falling on the rock surface to run back into the soil to keep plant roots cool and moist. If the rock slopes forward or is placed in a vertical position it will not gently direct water back to the plant roots, and the rain or irriga-

tion water will be lost entirely as it runs off, waterfall-style, into the garden below.

Set out the stones so you can examine their size, shape and any strata running through them. Starting at the bottom of the garden bed, place the foundation, or largest, rocks on their broadest base and tilt them slightly into the slope to direct rainwater toward the plant roots. Terrace the soil bed upward. Tamp soil firmly around 1/3 of each rock to set it in place. It may be a good idea to reserve some soil mix to add later as the level settles.

Regardless of garden style, 1/3 of each rock will be covered for stability, the soil mix will be from 15 cm to 30 cm deep in and around the rocks, and the gardener will need to experiment with plant placement to make plants fit the niches as they are created.

The small rock walls of the transformed Paulson garden almost vanish once the garden is planted and stepping stones, which repeat the rock used in the rock wall, are placed in the path of gravel mulch.

This small garden wall, built entirely of Rundle rock, takes shape before any soil is mixed or plants installed. A clearly outlined and defined space such as this is easily achieved in both small or large garden spaces. (PHOTOS BY CLIFF PAULSON)

Soil is prepared and backfilled into the created cracks in this Shaver–Strelau berm.

Plants fill the cracks and crannies provided in the Strelau–Shaver rock garden.

CHAPTER 5

Planting the Rock Garden

O NCE THE SITE HAS BEEN chosen and prepared, the soil blended and the rock placed according to your general plan, the very satisfying step of planting the rock garden begins. Before actually putting plants in the soil it is a good idea to arrange the plants in their pots around the garden, and, keeping in mind each plant's mature height, spread and color, step back and examine potential plantings from all angles. Make sure that forms and textures are varied enough to create interest and enough repetition is used to create continuity. For example, if seven tiny townsendias *(Townsendia parryi)* are placed between the crack created by two large rocks, three larger leaf bergenia *(Bergenia* spp.) might fill the space just behind.

The first specimens to be planted

Sedum (Hylotelephium ewersii) *resting against Rundle rock creates a stunning focal point. The leaves are like jewels as they emerge in spring. In summer they are toppped with pale pink flowers.*

153

Some saxifrages are so tiny that the whole plant can be placed in a crack in a rock. This Rocky Mountain native. Saxifraga oppositifolia, sits in a hole crafted in tufa and creates an unexpected point of interest for garden visitors.

are the largest rooted plants—evergreens and shrubs—which are sometimes set in place with the last of the rock. Such larger plants are controversial items in the rock garden because of fears the roots will consume and invade all the soil on the site. Some gardeners keep their rock gardens completely devoid of woody plants. Others· choose to keep the roots confined, bonsai style, in a landscape fabric bag or even in a nursery pot with the bottom cut out and the top well hidden.

In my rock garden several dwarf trees have been used but only after first excluding large full-scale shrubs from the site. The miniature trees include both evergreen and deciduous plants, native and culti-

vated. One, a small wild larch *(Larix laricina)* came from Churchill, Manitoba, via a team of botanists from Denmark and Iceland, who were on a cross-Canada collecting trip, looking for material for the reforestation of Iceland. My reward for providing bed and breakfast for these four botanists was a few bare-root larch trees. Although the larch looked like seedlings the botanists assured me they were at least 40 years old. An additional five years in the garden has doubled the size of the one remaining tree, which is wedged between rocks in a small south-facing crevice. I've made no attempt to restrict the roots of my woody plants in any way, but I do not hesitate to cut roots if they expand into regions I am working up for other smaller herbaceous plants. This helps maintain their dwarf stature. Woody plants, especially conifers, should have their roots disturbed as little as possible during planting.

The process of planting smaller herbaceous perennials in the rock garden is almost the same as planting other garden perennials. Remove the plant carefully from its pot and gently squeeze the rootball to remove some of the excess soil mix before placing it in the planting hole created with a small trowel. Do not set the crown of the plant deeper in the soil than it was in the pot. If a plant has become root-bound (with roots winding around the rootball), you may trim them to encourage growth after planting. Having placed the rootball at an angle in the hole, gently firm the soil around the rootball and top with 1" (2.5 cm) of fine gravel, turkey grit or crushed slate. The mulch will help to protect the plant from frost heaving, which occurs because the organic soil that many perennials are grown in shrinks and expands at a different rate than the amended rock garden soil. The problem will make itself apparent the following spring when plants are found with their roots exposed on top of the ground. Water each plant as it is placed and then water the entire garden when planting is complete. Continue a regimen of regular watering until your plants are well established, after which they will need watering only during extended dry spells.

Some plants require extra care in planting. Lewisias *(Lewisia* spp.), for instance, are often quite succulent in nature, where they grow in rock cracks and crevices. In the garden, therefore, they are best planted between two rocks with the crown at a steep angle, which prevents water from sitting on the plant crowns and rotting them. When in doubt always consult your local garden center for advice on special planting instructions.

The best times for planting are during mild spring weather, when the ground is easy to work, or in the early autumn, when there is suffi-

This native lewisia (Lewisia rediviva) *is so small a gardener needs to get on hands and knees to see it! With the plant only 1" (2.5 cm) or so across, the relatively huge flowers—up to 2" (5 cm) across— make this lewisia spectacular in a very miniaturized way.*

cient time for plants to become established before winter.

Smaller herbaceous perennials are generally purchased in 2 1/2" (6-cm) or 4" (10-cm) pots and are typically spaced 6–12" apart depending on mature spread. Some smaller mound plants may be placed as close as 4" (10 cm) apart, while the spreading ground covers are better spaced 12–18" (30–45 cm) apart. As a general rule expect to plant 10–20 specimens per 3 sq ft (1 sq m) of open garden. (The detailed plant list at the end of Chapter 2 describes plants by their growth habit, which will make it easier to calculate the total number of plants needed.)

As a general rule do not over-plant the garden. It's easy to cram

An often hybridized type of lewisia is Lewisia cotyledon. This extremely beautiful plant has one major disadvantage: it is often short-lived in the prairie garden.

for the roots and their beneficial *michorizae* (root associated fungus). A garden without adequate mulch is prone to severe frost heaving during the repeated freeze–thaw cycles common on the prairies during late fall and early spring.

Mulch's second practical benefit is in keeping soil moisture levels more uniform. Mulch holds moisture and humidity around the fine surface roots, which dry out and die if exposed to our intense prairie light and wind. A garden without adequate mulch may lose its minimal water reserve quickly.

Mulch's third practical benefit is in keeping the crowns of plants from sitting directly on moist soil. This is especially important when small plants accustomed to a dry, barren tundra or alpine environment are suddenly growing in a moister environment. Prolonged contact with wet soil will cause the lower leaves or even the whole crown of the plant to rot. A proper rock garden mulch will be dry to the touch on the upper surface within an hour of watering.

The fourth practical benefit of mulching is a reduction in competition from weeds.

The final benefit of mulching is aesthetic. Mulch creates a uniform look across the garden, linking the plants and rocks in a pleasing unified picture.

In our nonrock gardens we may use a compost, leaf mold or com-

in too many plants but better to let them grow into the garden rather than having to remove or cut back fast growers within a year or two. No matter how long you garden, there will always be a new plant discovery, and it's nice to have a place to put new acquisitions as you find them rather than always having to renovate or extend the garden.

Mulching the Rock Garden

Every garden on the prairies benefits from mulching, and rock gardens are no exception. Mulch's first practical benefit to prairie plants is its ability to keep soil temperatures more uniform—even cooler on occasion—than bare soil. This makes a more stable environment posted bark mulch to cover the root zone of perennials, shrubs or annual flowers. These organic mulches slowly break down or decompose. This contributes nutrients to the soil and gradually acidifies the soil, making nutrients more available. The various mulches useful to rock gardeners, however, are inorganic rather than organic and do not decompose or add nutrients over time.

In the rock garden the soil is purposely kept lean (or low in organic matter) so the plants stay small and compact. Inorganic mulches, usually rock-based, may affect soil chemistry as elements leach into the soil, but they won't affect its fertility. Suggested rock garden mulches include fine washed gravels, rock chips, coarse silica grit or limestone grit (also sold as poultry or turkey grit). These fine gravels are the same as materials worked into the blended rock garden soil except that they are left on the surface in a layer 1" (2.5 cm) deep. To determine the mulch quantities required, use the same process described for calculating soil quantities (see page 144).

The best permanent inorganic mulches will keep the soil at or near its optimum pH level of below 7. Ideally, the mulch chosen will also be attractive and will not cause extra work for you in the years to come. Avoid choosing mulches that will show natural debris too easily. One of my most enduring memories

is being asked as a student (over twenty years ago) to selectively remove pine needles from a pure white rock mulch used as a formal element in a Japanese garden. Selectively removing anything from a loose and formal material such as white rock is a formidable task. In a formal garden it is probably best to have surfaces that can be hosed off.

If rocks are used as a mulch, it is best to make use of the same very fine washed rocks or pebbles that have been incorporated into the soil mix. As the regular garden operations of weeding or plant removal and division are carried out, the surface mulch will be indirectly incorporated into the soil, and every now and then a little more mulch may be

The garden edge in any garden is extremely important. A brick border seldom does the job of keeping out invading grass. It is better to combine the brick with a plastic edging or to cement the brick into place on the turf side of the joint.

Seasonal color unfolds with the reliable ground-cover blue spruce (Picea pungens 'Glauca procumbens') in the background, a dianthus cultivar in the middle and the fairly new motherlode juniper (Juniperus horizontalis 'Motherlode') up front just after it was planted from its 4" (10 cm) pot. Within a season this plant had doubled in size.

added to areas that have become thin. Keep a small reserve of mulch on hand. If a fresh look is needed, the whole garden can be remulched with a thin layer of the original mulch used. Alpine rock gardens look especially authentic with a top layer of washed grit, gravel or Rundle stone. While other gardeners in other styles of gardens employ fabric liners between the soil and mulch, I have found they don't ultimately save time and they inevitably become exposed and unsightly.

Occasionally, within the context of a shady woodland rock garden, organic mulches such as composted bark may be used instead of rock. These usually lower pH and will gradually establish a pH equilibrium in the soil lower than what is common for prairie soil. Overall, this is a very good thing because slightly acidic soils are good for all plants. Prairie rock gardeners need not fear using bark or evergreen-based mulches because most prairie soils have pH levels of neutral or above neutral and will benefit from a small addition of acidic material.

Again, as work is carried on in the woodland rock garden, the finely shredded composted bark materials will become incorporated into the soil and will improve its structure and chemical properties. Every three to five years, the mulch may be topped up to refresh the look. Keep a small supply of material on hand for spot applications after weeding or routine maintenance has left the soil exposed.

Suggested rock garden mulches are sold under various trade names or by size. The following are examples of acceptable prairie rock garden mulches. They are listed here exactly as they appear at bulk landscape suppliers:

1/2" NATURAL

Round-edged washed gravel with the largest particles passing through a 1/2" screen.

3/8" PEA GRAVEL

Washed gravel with edges somewhat more rounded because it is screened rather than crushed to size.

7 MM GYRA SAND CHIPS

Fine, washed, sharp-edged pea gravel with flat edges resulting from crushing before screening.

SIL 9

Round-edged reddish brown pebbles (also called turkey grit or red-brown granite pebbles) about the same size as the 7 mm gyra.

10 MM TAN ROCK

A sand-colored washed gravel with rounded edges.

10 MM RUNDLE SAND

An unwashed dark brown-black gravel that tends to settle and pack, almost creating a crusting on the surface (Rundle sand should be thoroughly washed before it is used for mulching).

#1 TO #3 CHICKEN GRIT

A fine, bright grey-to-white rock sold in bags at animal feed stores (it's bright color makes it an unpopular choice for many rock gardens, but it is useful to top up pots of seedling plants).

ALPINE MULCH

Finely screened and composted bark (this dark brown low-nutrient mulch will grey with age and is especially suited to woodland or shade rock gardens).

A simple display of white iris (Iris cv.) and the common perrenial snow in summer (Cerastium tomentosum) provide seasonal color. This moment of white blooms in a somewhat shady public garden is a joy to come across.

CHAPTER 6

Seasonal Care of the Rock Garden

THE PHRASE *LOW MAINTENANCE* could have been coined with rock gardens in mind. If you have securely set the rock in place, selected hardy plants and properly mulched the surface, your rock garden will require very little care. While larger plants in more traditional gardens need staking, regular feeding, watering, weeding, cultivating and dividing, very few of these typical maintenance practices are needed in the rock garden. The dwarf or drought-tolerant mountain and prairie species common to prairie rock gardens tend to be self-cleaning and so require little dead-heading. The amended soil conditions contribute to a relatively slow rate of growth and thus reduce the need for dividing. Water use is minimized because rockery plants often have water-holding or heat-deflecting characteristics (survival mecha-

161

A couple of classic mistakes were made in this unfortunate space. First, the rocks are not used in any way that might simulate nature—instead they are perched on end tombstone style. Secondly, all the rocks are close in size and form, which is too much repetition even in a good garden. Finally, like all gardens, rock gardens need some basic maintenance. If there is very little time to maintain your space make sure to eradicate weedy grasses from the area before it is planted and then edge the garden with an impermeable material such as concrete to prevent the encroachment of weeds.

nisms carried over from their earlier lives in mountain crevices or dry prairies), and water also is held in by mulch. And unless you insist on growing rockery plants entirely from snowy habitats, most will not need special winter cover or extraordinary care. They will likely survive even if the snow cover blows away with Chinooks or spring winds.

Except for nominal attention—occasional pruning, replacing of winter-killed plants, topping up mulch, occasional propagating of plants and infrequent weeding—the rock garden pretty much looks after itself.

Winter Care

Rock garden plants overwinter well if there is good snow cover and few freeze-thaw cycles—conditions that prevail for most of the prairies except the windy Chinook belt. At

their most extreme, prolonged Chinooks may force high alpine specimens into bloom, which occurred during the Winter Olympics in February 1988. While the Olympic staff were busy making snow, rock gardeners were enjoying early hepatica *(Hepatica* spp.) blooms.

To protect plants from frost, special blankets may be purchased to keep your garden under cover, but they are not usually attractive, especially in highly visible front-yard settings. If frost-heaving causes plants to pop out, do not just press them back in the ground. Dig a new hole and replant them.

Spring Care

Spring is the ideal time to divide or propagate any plants in need of attention. Many early flowering plants, such as drumstick primulas *(Primula denticulata)*, which are

often in bloom by late April, may be easily divided after they bloom by digging them out and gently tugging apart the loose clumps of small plantlets. These individual plantlets are then reset at the same depth at which they were growing. Beware, however, of dividing all your plants at once, since a rare plunging temperature may kill the works.

With other spring bloomers such as Auricula primulas *(Primula auricula)*, it is best to take cuttings from the largest plants immediately after they flower rather than trying to divide the plant. These plants get leggy as they age, when the short-lived evergreen leaves die back, leaving a rather long naked stalk on top of the soil with tufts of leaves at the end. A small cutting is made with a sharp knife immediately after the plant blooms, and this cutting is stripped of its lower leaves, then pushed right back in to the soil,

where it will root within a few months. Because primulas are quite succulent, they don't need any special care during this rooting period unless a heat wave hits in early spring. In this case place a small wooden shingle or other shade material on the south side of the cutting to give it some midday shade while it is rooting.

If the leaves of your primula plant resemble lettuce more than cabbage, they will probably not multiply as easily by cuttings. Many of the excellent garden primulas for early spring color in the rock garden do not have the fleshy leaves of the auricula group. These soft-leaved forms are better multiplied by division or are easily started from seed rather than cuttings.

Another spring bloomer you may consider propagating is the lovely blue gentian *(Gentian acaulis)*. Gardeners lucky enough to have

LEFT: Another view of a mossy saxifrage, in this case the cultivar Rozenzwerg.

RIGHT: Adonis vernalis—also known as spring adonis—are an excellent fine-textured choice for a prairie garden if they have at least partial to half a day of shade.

LEFT: The common but reliable auricula primula (Primula auricula) isn't the first in bloom each spring, but it definitely blooms in May and has a long season of color.

RIGHT: Primula auricula 'Dale's Red' has become a favorite of mine with its long-lasting pink flowers in spring and its sturdy fleshy leaves that seem indestructible.

them will soon have people asking for cuttings. These gentians gradually creep out to form large mats of glossy green leaves with brilliant blue trumpet-shaped flowers standing up at least 1.5" (4 cm) above the foliage. Small rooted sections may be extracted at the edge of the mat for potting or replanting in another part of the garden. Extract these small sections before they bloom in May.

Other plants benefiting from division include ornamental onions *(Allium* spp.). Every three to five years, lift and separate the existing bulbs in late summer. Pussytoes *(Antennaria rosea)* can be divided any time more plants are needed. Other good candidates include windflower *(Anemone sylvestris)*, columbine *(Aquilegia* spp. and cvs.), fern leaf bleeding hearts *(Dicentra eximia)*, rockcress *(Arabis caucasica)*, species tulips *(Tulipa tarda)*,

campanulas *(Campanula* spp.), and corydalis *(Corydalis* cvs.).

Other plants are easily multiplied by cuttings. Try taking cuttings of the various saxifrages *(Saxifraga* cvs.), dianthus *(Dianthus* cvs.), mountain avens *(Dryas octopetala)*, and fleshy-leaved primulas such as *Primula auricula, Primula marginata* and *Primula hirsuta*.

Plants likely to spread by seed are the easiest multipliers of all. Simply wait and watch for small seedlings—which sometimes don't resemble the adult plant in the early stages. Plants seen spreading from seed in the prairie rock garden include hepatica *(Hepatica* spp.), columbine *(Aquilegia* spp.), dianthus *(Dianthus* spp.) poppies *(Papaver* spp.), and townsendia *(Townsendia parryi)*. I have also discovered seedlings of fleabane *(Erigeron compositus)*, moss campion *(Silene acaulis)*, corydalis *(Corydalis* spp.), species tulip *(Tulipa tarda)* and blue-eyed grass *(Sisyrinchium montanum)* in my garden.

Mid- to late spring also is the ideal time to harden off and plant seedlings started indoors during the winter. Because many rockery plants are sturdy and cold-tolerant, they can easily be acclimatized to the outdoors when they are small.

Finally, spring is the time to top up mulch in areas of the rock garden wherever it has become thin. While you do, it's useful to look near favorite plants for small seedlings you may have overlooked last autumn, especially from varieties that are almost impossible to collect from seed. A particularly frustrating example is hepatica *(Hepatica* spp.), the gorgeous early-blooming purple plant suited to almost full-shade prairie gardens. The seeds of hepatica seem to be expelled a short distance from the mother plant just before you expect it to ripen. While self-cleaning plants such as these are wonderful to have in the garden, the mother plants are so slow growing that it will be hard to satisfy your need for more plants by waiting for divisions alone. The seeds, if missed, may fall between the gaps in the gravel mulch and sit dormant for a few months or even seasons. When they suddenly germinate, you may accidentally remove them because the seedlings' leaves are completely different from the mature plant's and

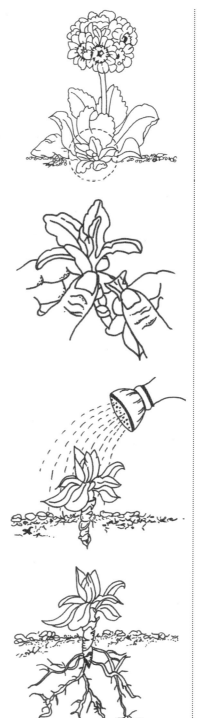

PROPAGATING PRIMULAS: Wait until just after flowering to remove a section of a fleshy-leaved primula (such as the Primula auricula shown).

Remove a newer, younger side shoot with a sharp knife. Then remove the leaves from the lower portion of the stem.

Plunge the new cutting directly into the garden and water in immediately. If it is unseasonably hot, provide the cutting with some shade.

By autumn expect it to be well rooted and established. It may be potted or moved to its final position once rooted. It should bloom the following spring.
(ILLUSTRATION BY KATHERINE VINISH)

LEFT: A brilliant choice for bloom in the early spring garden is hepatica (Hepatica spp.), also known as liverleaf.

RIGHT: A white form of hepatica (Hepatica spp.) is also showy early in the spring.

are often ignored or accidentally weeded out.

If you persevere and leave unknown seedlings in place in the garden, they may be dug as small clumps in the late spring or even early summer and potted up or transplanted to another position as they are found. This small task of looking for and moving seedlings is quite a fun event. In the case of certain plants such as Parry's townsendia *(Townsendia parryi)*, the seedlings themselves are the key to survival of the plant in your garden. The main plant is very short-lived, often dying after it blooms, but it almost always leaves a good supply of seed and subsequent seedlings behind. The seedlings place themselves in generous and broad swaths, supplying many new plants to the mature rock garden without any extra effort on your part. While some gardeners

look for and save seeds, it is far easier to allow plants to reseed themselves in place in the garden. It may be best to delay any efforts at weeding until such time as you have a better idea of what rock garden plant seedlings are emerging.

Aside from being time for maintenance and propagation, spring is the time for community plant exchanges so take some cuttings to share with other enthusiasts.

Summer Care

Summer maintenance in the rock garden is straight forward, involving the routine deadheading of spent blooms. To do this effectively you must distinguish between plants that self-seed and those that don't. Self-cleaning plants drop their flower petals quickly and the seeds dispense. No maintenance is required because they don't need to be deadheaded. Keep your shears handy to deadhead those plants that don't self-seed or that self-seed so prolifically that you wish to limit or reduce their numbers in the garden.

Highly invasive plants require more maintenance and leave the gardener with two choices: leave them at the nursery or learn to deal with their nature. If a plant reproduces by energetically reseeding, be reasonably diligent in clipping off the dead and dying flowers to prevent seeds from forming. Most dianthus are in this category. If the plant spreads by its roots, the decision to keep it or not is a little more complicated. One example of a probable keeper is the small creeping bluebell known as fairies' thimbles *(Campanula cochleariifolia)*. This delicate little plant spills from Rundle walls or creeps from between cracks in rock walls with a burst of blue that can't be matched. Gardeners who have publicly insisted that fairies' thimbles are too aggressive somehow leave it in their own gardens to great effect. You will need to monitor its spread and pull out or remove plant portions that go beyond where you want them. In my small space I haven't found room for this plant but have included its less pushy double-flowered form *Campanula cochleariifolia* 'Elizabeth Oliver.' This delightful plant may be dug as a rooted offset in spring before it blooms or purchased from a nursery.

An aggressive plant I have less

A third cultivar of hepatica (Hepatica transylvanica) illustrates the range of color in this delicate spring blooming species.

tolerance for is yarrow *(Achillea millefolium)*. Although it is pretty in bloom it spreads so aggressively that it squeezes out all plants in its path, becoming entrenched throughout the garden in just a few short years. I do not use yarrow in a mixed planting bed among other less aggressive plants. Instead, use it where drought and low maintenance are the only concerns and give it the whole bed.

Aside from deadheading and control of invasive species, summer maintenance will involve only the most occasional weeding. Dandelions are alpine plants and love rock gardening soil, so dig them out as soon as they are spotted.

Probably the most obvious summer work is the task of watering. In many cases it is best to under water than to over water because several of our prized plants have fleshy, even succulent, leaves and are tolerant of dry soil. Keep an eye on heavier water users by looking for signs of wilting or by physically pushing your fingers into the mulch and soil below to check for dampness. A thorough watering every two to three weeks is all the extra care the rock garden needs.

Autumn Care

If there is a single cardinal rule of rock garden soils it is to keep them frozen in the winter—not to try to prevent them from freezing. Do this by watering well in the autumn and avoiding mulches or plant covers that prevent thorough freezing. If you feel compelled to cover your garden for winter protection, it is important that you be patient until the soil is frozen. And then, above all, avoid the "once only mistake" new prairie gardeners sometimes make when they add a wheat, oat or barley straw mulch to their gardens in the autumn. I call it the "once only mistake" because it causes such grief that gardeners never forget it and never do it again. Straw mulches contain large numbers of weed and grain seeds, and the resulting seedlings are difficult to remove in the spring. If the straw is applied before the soil is frozen and a snowfall comes soon after, you also create a marvelous habitat for mice and voles, which will create an entire network of paths and tunnels bigger than Sim City. Hardy plants

not allowed to freeze and go dormant may rot beneath any mulch applied to protect them.

Patience to wait until the ground is frozen doesn't mean that you shouldn't water in the fall. It is a good idea to have the rock garden go into the winter with the soil moistened. Moist soil (not completely saturated and soggy) will allow air between soil particles in a well-structured rock garden soil. While it is true that roots need oxygen to respire, the cool temperatures will decrease respiration needs. If soil is moist as it freezes, you will achieve the greatest overwintering success and won't have to worry about winter watering.

Never assume that late-autumn watering takes care of every area in the rock garden equally. Zones under or near evergreens will dry out much quicker than other areas and will need to be checked more than once late in the season before the ground is completely frozen. Once the ground is frozen, watering should be avoided since it may cause the soil to thaw and could increase the possibility of frost heaving.

Cutting back plant tops before winter snow has always been a debatable point among rock gardeners. If the tops are left standing they may catch snow and provide some protection to the plant crown. They also may provide food for fall and winter foraging wildlife. In my

The creeping baby's breath (Gypsophila repens) is perfectly in scale with a lichen-covered fieldstone at the end of the garden.

garden pheasants come by in little troops to nibble at the fine gravel and to search for seeds left on plants.

If plant tops are cut well back—especially if this is done early—the crowns may be exposed to drying winter winds and desiccation, so if you want to cut back your rock garden plants for aesthetic purposes, patience is again a virtue because the difference between *early* and *late* is an evening snowfall or suddenly plunging temperatures with no snow cover.

Because of the unexpected temperature shifts in the prairie Chinook belt in winter, it is common for some gardeners to cover their special alpine plants in the late fall after the soil has frozen. Most of the rock garden plants listed in this book, however, including the evergreens, are known for their hardiness and do not need special care to overwinter successfully in a garden that has been mulched. Evergreens add four-season interest to the rock garden, and this is lost if you choose varieties that require gunnysack wraps to survive the winter.

Glossary

Alpine

Usually a high elevation plant but very similar to arctic plants in form and adaptations. May thrive in various alpine habitats including cliffs, meadows, moraine, scree or bog.

Cultivars

Specially selected plants with specific and definable characteristics. They are either the result of a garden selection (a keen gardener or breeder spotting an unusual form) or a determined cross between species. In this second case, it is possible that several clones or cultivars may be named from a single cross. Either way, named cultivars are propagated to maintain them as identical clones so that their predefined characteristics are retained. This means they are usually not shared as seed but as a stem or root cuttings. Commercially, they are often multiplied by tissue culture.

A cultivar is identified by a capital letter and single quotation marks such as *Arabis caucasica* 'Variegata.' The name *Variegata* would not normally be used in isolation because this descriptive word could be applied to all kinds of plants with variegated leaves. Sometimes the abbreviation *cv.* is used to describe a single cultivar or *cvs.* to describe several. If, for instance, there is more than one known or recommended cultivar of columbines, you might see *Aquilegia* cvs. used to describe the group.

Krummholz

A small clump of trees in the subalpine region (or merging into the alpine), where a group of spruce or fir grow together in a clump as a form of protection for one another. The overall form of the Krummholz is a pyramid with the smaller evergreens on the edge of the clump providing shelter from the wind for the taller plants in the middle.

Saxatile

Plants described as saxatile grow in or among rocks in high or low elevation. These may be sun- or shade-tolerant plants of any description, their only requirement being that they are associated with rock in nature

Scree

An area of loose gravel and small rock, usually in a mountain setting, and often at the base of a rock wall or at the edge of a glacier. Plants described as scree plants tolerate very poor soil with a high gravel content.

Associations

Gardening with rocks and the plants known to grow among them becomes addictive. Once the locally available plants have been tried, the keen gardener starts to look further afield for sources of plants and seeds not as commonly found. Membership in various rock garden societies gives a steady source of information and also usually provides a source of free seed through society exchanges. Some of the best groups to investigate are included here.

Associations

Alpine Garden Society (AGS)
AGS Centre
Avon Bank
Pershore
Worcestershire WR10 3JP
United Kingdom

Calgary Rock and Alpine Garden
Society (CRAGS)
Attention: Sheila Paulson,
Membership
6960 Leaside Drive SW
Calgary, AB T3E 6H5
Canada

North American Rock Garden
Society (NARGS)
PO Box 67
Millwood, NY 10546
USA

Scottish Rock Garden Club
Attention: Mr. B. Ingham,
Membership Secretary
Sandwood Cottage, Greenbank,
Eggleston, Barnard Castle DL12 0BQ
Scotland

Sempervivum Society
11, Wingletye Road
Burgess Hill, Sussex RH159HR
England

Books and Periodicals

Balzer, Donna, ed. "Soils in the Rock Garden." *CRAGS Newsletter* 2.3 (February 1998): 6.

Bentley, C.F. and J.A. Robertson. *Soils and Fertilizers for Gardens and Lawns.* Edmonton: University of Alberta Press, 1977.

Foster, H. Lincoln. *Rock Gardening: A Guide to Growing Alpines and Other Wildflowers in the American Garden.* Portland: Timber Press, 1982.

Griffiths, Mark, ed. "Index of Garden Plants." *The New Royal Horticultural Society Dictionary.* Portland: Timber Press, 1994.

Harris, Paul and Terry Warke. *The Prairie Water Garden.* Red Deer: Red Deer Press, 1998.

Ingwersen, Will. *Alpine and Rock Plants.* Great Britain: J.M. Dent and Sons, 1983.

Innes, Clive. *Alpines: The Illustrated Dictionary.* Portland: Timber Press, 1995.

Lowe, Duncan. *Growing Alpines in Raised Beds, Troughs, and Tufa.* Great Britain: B.T. Batsford, 1991.

NARGS. *Rock Garden Plants of North America.* Portland: Timber Press, 1996.

Schacht, Wilhelm. *Rock Gardens.* Portland: Timber Press, 1981.

Stevens, David. *The Garden Design Sourcebook: The Essential Guide to Garden Materials and Structures.* Vancouver: Raincoast Books, 1995.

Plant and Seed Sources

Plant Sources

Edward's Garden Centre
Attention: Hildur Childs
7948 Bowness Road NW
Calgary, AB T3B 0H2
Canada
Tel: 403-288-9638
Fax: 403-288-9643
A small garden center with interesting shrubs and alpines.

Holes Garden Centre
101 Bellerose Drive
St. Albert, AB T8N 8N8
Canada
Tel: 780-419-6800
Fax: 780-459-6042
Order desk: 1-888-884-6537
E-mail: info@holesonline.com
Web: www.holesonline.com
A very large garden center with a perennial plant specialist interested in rock garden plants. They also offer mail order services.

Rundlewood Gardens
1643 Altadore Ave SW
Calgary, AB T2T 2P8
Canada
Tel: (403) 243-9982
Fax: (403) 243-9982
e-mail: rundlewd@cadvision.com
Tel (for catalogue): 403-243-9982
A small homebased nursery with much wisdom and expertise.

Siskiyou Rare Plant Nursery
2825 Cummings Road
Medford, OR 97501
USA
Tel: 541-772-6846
Fax: 541-772-4917

The Perennial Gardens
13139 – 224 Street
Maple Ridge, BC V4R 2P6
Canada
Tel: 604-467-4218
Fax: 604-467-3181
E-mail: info@perennialgardener.com
Web: www.perennialgardener.com
A very broad catalogue. Mail order services are available.

Seed Sources

Exchanges
Karmic Exotic Nursery
Box 146
Shelburne, ON L0N 1S0
Tel: (519) 925-3906
Canada

Rocky Mountain Rare Plants
1706 Deerpath Road
Franktown, CO 80116-9462
USA